Final ——y

Chic Vol. 2

How to be savvy with
money in tough times,
cultivate your rich lady
lifestyle, and live
fabulously for less

FIONA FERRIS

Contents

~~

Chapter 1.

My story

Ever since I worked as a secretary for financial planning advisors in my twenties I developed a love for personal finance. I know the phrase 'personal finance' can sound so dry and... boring. But somehow, during that time a switch was flicked for me, and it became exciting and something that I loved to read about, and watch! A few years after that I devoured Oprah's *Debt Diet* series when it was on her show.

This focus meant I went from being someone who applied to the bank for a personal loan for a small stereo as a teen (what was I thinking!) and came out with a credit card which I never quite seemed to pay off, to a debt-free millionaire in my fifties. In between these times, let's say from ages twenty to fifty, I learned *a lot*. I learned what made me feel stressed and upset, and what helped me feel relaxed and at peace.

Of course, 'money can't buy you happiness', but having enough brings you peace of mind, a feeling of lightness and joy, and the nice feeling that you'll be okay a.k.a. safety, security and stability.

It wasn't until I was in my thirties though that I really got my head switched on. I'd just met a lovely boyfriend that I could see a future with, and a year or two after meeting we started living together. Soon after that he opened a business – a shoe store – in partnership with former customers of his when he was a footwear sales representative.

Within a few months I'd left my job and joined him in this venture, and we worked together there for twelve years, marrying along the way.

A few years into the business we bought out our business partners, and unbeknownst to us, the Global Financial Crisis (or GFC) happened around the same time – circa 2007. That taught us *even more*. We were 100% responsible for the business, and all of a sudden the bills were a lot more than what was coming into the cash register.

We actually saw the money tap turn off 6-12 months sooner than the GFC hit the news, and it was very worrying. Looking back, it had obviously hit retail sooner than other areas such as housing. But of course, we didn't know any of that back then. All we knew was that we couldn't pay our business bills in full each month like we were used to doing.

It was a humbling experience to explain to our footwear suppliers that we didn't have enough to be up-to-date with our accounts, but we said we would pay what we could until we were caught up.

Understandably they were not happy, and two companies in particular played hardball. Perhaps they had seen it all before with other retailers and didn't want to be left with debts they had no way of recouping. Totally fair! But in time even they came around, as they saw us making extra payments towards our debt with them, and several months later we were fully paid up, and back in good standing with everyone.

This was seventeen years ago and neither of us have forgotten the horrible feeling of disappointing people and not being able to pay our bills temporarily. But afterwards we had the wonderful feeling of coming through it, and we committed to *never letting ourselves get in that position again*.

Back then, we were renting a small house for ourselves and our two cats. We hadn't bought a home yet because we didn't want to have the financial stress of two loans to pay (did I mention we had borrowed a big chunk of change to buy our business partners out?)

But we kept our business loan current as we paid off our suppliers, continued trading well, learned how to be savvy with our stock management, and lived a good life on a very small budget. This experience was *how* we learned to live a good life on a very small budget.

In 2011 we bought our first home together having paid off our business loan. We had scraped together a deposit, through sheer 'living below our means' and working hard. We went without a lot of things but still had fun. We made our own fun! When we got married in 2008, we had very little money, so it was a wedding for less than 40 people including us, and we had two days off work. We didn't go on our honeymoon until almost six years later!

All of this, including how we paid off that home in full within five years is detailed in my book 'Financially Chic', published in 2016. We still lived in the city then, but we were making plans to move to the small provincial area where I'd grown up, simply because we wanted to try something different – to live a gentler, more relaxed life. We'd had twelve years working in our shoe store and saw that retail was changing, with internet shopping, and brands opening up their own stores around us.

We wanted to slow the pace from our 'big city life' to a smaller country-style existence. So in 2017 we did just that, selling our business and then our home, packing up the cats in their carriers secured on the back seat of our thrifty Toyota Camry and headed down country, six hours away during a rare snow-storm! It was quite the trip and all four of us were happy to arrive in our new hometown, then move into our newly purchased country home the next day and meet the furniture truck that had followed us down. Our new adventure had begun! Looking back, it was all possible because we embraced an era of thrift and discipline. We still had a long way to go but it was already paying off.

Enter 2024. Earlier this year, my husband Paul was six months into a new job, and the economy was looking grim. He worked in car sales, and virtually from the day he started, new car sales started bombing. He'd previously worked as a brand manager for a different car dealership since we'd moved to our new town, so he knew the car business well.

At the beginning of 2024 his new boss talked to him and said there may have to be cutbacks in staff. As it turned out Paul's position and a couple of others were made redundant.

In addition to this, my book sales had gone down too – virtually since the first day of 2024. As with our shoe sales, the tap had turned off, not fully but by about half. I think for my books it was a combination of not having released a new title in a while, and also about people cutting back on discretionary items such as buying books. Everyone was finding it tough and not just us.

All this to say, our household income dropped by more than 75%. Yes, you heard right, 75%. Which means we had about 25% of what we had been used to. At first, we weren't too worried because of a number of factors (despite it being a big shock that Paul had lost his job):

- Our home was fully paid off so our only outgoings for shelter were water, rates, insurance and maintenance.

- We'd upgraded the outside by painting our home, having it fully re-roofed, replacing old cracked shabby looking concrete with tiles, and had a new patio pergola built. However, it was all paid for with money we'd saved beforehand. I can only imagine the stress if we'd borrowed money from the bank for this costly work.

- And, we've always had 'cheap hobbies'. We still enjoy cooking at home, watching movies, reading, going for a stroll around town and not buying anything except perhaps lunch or a coffee. Yes, we do have vacations, but these are paid for with 'current money', not on a credit card or 'future money'. We were lucky enough to go on an all-expenses paid work trip to Hawaii last year, but before that our last overseas trip was in 2019.

Even with our paid-off home and thrifty ways though, a few months later when I did some sums on our accounts, I could see we were spending a lot more than was coming in. We had a savings account where the balance fluctuated throughout the month, but when I looked at the balance on the same day each month, it was declining. The trend was downwards, which wasn't surprising given our circumstances. So even though we had a semi-thrifty lifestyle (we'd been able to upgrade from 'thrifty'), we needed to make some changes.

Early on we'd made the decision that Paul

wouldn't rush out and take the first job he saw. We are older now and enjoying relaxing a little after our earlier days of literally watching every penny and working seven days a week between us. He wasn't in a position to retire, we're only in our early fifties, but we did have to make some changes.

In this book, I share with you what we have done, and my thoughts on the mindset that has made us financially successful up until this point. No, we're not as rich as some, but I do feel very fortunate to be in the position we are. We have a roof over our heads, and within reason we can buy what we want.

No matter your financial situation, I think you will find inspiration, practical tips, and new ideas to try in this book. It's never too early or too late to rejig your money life. I will show you how it can be enjoyable and fun. I promise! I am not a financial expert and none of what I say is intended as financial advice. But I believe I have plenty to share with you that may enhance your own financial situation.

My goal is that the money you have spent on this book will be *your best investment ever*, and that the reading of it becomes a pivotal point in your financial happiness and feelings of wealth and abundance. May the purchase price be returned to you one-hundred-fold!

With all my best to you from my cozy home office in beautiful Hawke's Bay, New Zealand,

Chapter 2.

Calm your panicked mind

Perhaps your mortgage payments have already increased, and interest rates still seem to be rising. Or your rent has gone up and it's cut into your wallet *and* your serenity. And let's not even mention grocery prices, they're out of control!

Before you start spiralling, look at things objectively. You have a roof over your head and you're not in danger of being homeless, right? Right. Okay. So that's a good start. You have a calm, cozy home or apartment to live in. Or a room that you rent. Yes?

If your abode seems ho-hum now, remember the excitement you had for it when you first moved in. Look at your home from this perspective and anchor in the feeling of appreciation and newness from that time.

Or imagine how someone would be *thrilled* to be where you are right now, in the place where you live, and even paying the bills you do.

No-one likes 'having money taken away from them' with no extra benefit, but it's just a fact of life right now. Everything is becoming more expensive, from food and housing to fuel and utility bills. Everyone is in the same boat.

To help you feel even a tiny bit better:

- Try to **appreciate what you do have**. The food in your kitchen, the clothes in your closet, and the place where you live. Go right down to the smallest things if you need to!

- Know that **everyone is affected** to varying degrees. It really seems to be a global concern right now, with few countries unaffected. And you will also have many people close to you that are freaked out too – family, friends, and work colleagues.

- Know that **hard times can't last forever**. You can make changes to help yourself out now, and when things aren't so tough, you may even emerge triumphant. What you choose to do now can set you up for a bright future.

Be that supportive friend to yourself, soothing yourself and helping you see that things aren't as doom-filled as they might feel. Remind yourself often that, 'This is only temporary' and 'I can do strong things'.

By making these 'thought adjustments' your worried mind will hopefully feel a little calmer. And from this more grounded place you will be able to work out concrete ideas for yourself. Ideas to start making a few changes because *every little thing helps*.

Creating positive thoughts and making tiny adjustments will also help you step out of *worry mode* and into *solution mode*. Because it's when we start spiralling that we feel the most hopeless and helpless. Everything seems terrible!

But that's not strictly true is it?

There will be glimmers of hope, areas in which you are doing well, and also at least a few ways in which you can make things better.

The periods of my life when money has been truly tight were also my greatest times of transformation. Looking back I can see this, but at the time I was scared witless and felt so vulnerable. I made necessary changes though, sometimes big ones, and those experiences have shaped how I am today, which is better with money than when I was younger. There were valuable lessons learned!

And so it is in this current time when our household income has been severely trimmed. We are okay overall because we've built a strong financial foundation, but it was a time, again, when we identified quite a few expenditures which were there just because we'd set them up, and we let them go on week after week. It was the impetus of Paul's redundancy that got us to look at them objectively and decide which recurring expenditures were important to us and which we could live without.

It's actually an exercise that we would all do well to address regularly – at least every year, but when things are carrying on as normal it's definitely easy to forget to do this.

It helps to take a zoomed-out perspective and view the big picture too because sometimes we can be so deep in it, that we can't see that. A funny saying I heard recently said 'you can't read the label from inside the box' and it's true! We've got to get out of the box!

Just know that 'it's always darkest before the dawn'. This saying has often soothed me when I've had circular negative thoughts about a situation.

I'm not trying to trivialize any pain, financial or otherwise that you are going through, it's just something I have found for myself. That things always work out! And it feels good to believe that they are working in my favour too, no matter how hard it was at the time. Like when my first husband dumped me, that totally sucked, but now I'm so happy he did. Some sixteen years later we met up for a coffee after my dad died and I actually thanked him for leaving me so that I could go on to meet someone more well-suited. And I meant it with love!

So look upon this time as the pressure that will make your life into a diamond. A beautiful, sparkling diamond steeped in richness. How's that for a visual to look forward to?

Your Financially Chic inspirational ideas:

- Make a gratitude list of **all that's good in your life** right now. Completely ignore the bad and make a list as long as you can of all the goodness, pleasure, and what areas you are already 'wealthy' in.

- **Talk to like-minded people** and feel out if they are interested in sharing their worries. You don't need to go into specifics, but maybe you'll even ask someone close to you to give you a pep talk. I asked my brother to do this for me once and it was actually really lovely. He tried his best to pump me up and I was grateful for it!

- **Be your own cheerleader**. Write out a pep talk or speak softly and tell yourself, *Things will be okay, it's just a temporary situation, you are resourceful and can work things out. Imagine if what is happening right now is for your highest good and you will look back in wonder one day at how perfectly everything has worked out.*

- Brainstorm ideas for yourself on **how you can feel good** about your current situation and what little changes you could possibly make right now. If you find this hard to come up with, imagine a friend has asked you for your help. Viewing a challenge as if it is someone else's always gives me great ideas. You can act as the impartial coach!

Chapter 3.

Elevate your mindset

Okay, so you know you want to change things up. You want to worry less about your financial situation and focus on building wealth, even in the current economic climate. You can see others doing this, even if most people are complaining. You have decided that you want to be one of the success stories, not a cautionary tale.

You don't want to wake up at night anxious about rising interest rates or spiralling inflation. But neither do you want to knuckle down or go on a money diet that promises to be hard and dry and miserable. No thank you! Instead, you have decided that you are going to make this a fun game. You are going to live your best life, build personal wealth, and be an inspiration to others in the way you live.

You are committed to learning about – and proving to yourself – how it can be fun to spend less and be creative. Because it's fun to feel *relaxed and happy,* and not *stressed and pinched*! You don't want to feel worried about your mortgage payments going up and how you're going to cope with that.

You are ready to change your mindset from consumption and shopping, to making the most of what you already have, appreciating it, and building up financial wealth for the future of yourself and your family. You are willing to change what you get a kick out of!

You want to learn how to make it fun to be frugal – I promise this is not an oxymoron. And if the word frugal has negative connotations for you, choose another: careful, savvy, economical, prudent, unwasteful, canny, sparing, or meticulous. I like the thought of being *exquisite* with money, or *elegant* with money. Doesn't *financial elegance* have a nice ring to it? Imagine choosing to be financially elegant as your new mindset?

Know that you *can* 'live beyond your means' and it all starts with your mindset. You are ready to romanticize frugality, be penny-wise, practice voluntary simplicity or whatever phrase rings your bell. You look forward to your fresh state of mind and how it is going to serve you, and you know you can't wait to get started by the time you finish reading this book, or maybe even before.

I remember how good it felt when I flicked the switch and viewed money as fun and easy instead of stressful and scary. I felt more in control of my destiny and it was such a soothing feeling. It was also exciting, because I felt empowered and emboldened. I was the one driving the bus now!

How do you do it though? How do you change a lifetime of conditioning, and believing what your parents (and other people) say about money? Sometimes it takes serious journalling and digging into what those inherited beliefs are.

My father always said he never tried to make money from his hobbies, because it would ruin the enjoyment for him. And what happened with me? I started writing books based on all the topics I love. My 'work' doesn't feel like work. It is certainly more fun than the office jobs I used to work at and think of as necessary. So what my dad decided was true for him, I have decided is *not* true for me. But if I had just blindly believed what he did, I might not be here writing this book today.

Or maybe you don't need to dig deep; it might be a quote or idea or book that flicks the switch for you like it did for me. Once you find the flavour that motivates, excites and inspires you, there is no looking back. You're on your way!

And I think that's what a lot of people don't get, it's not just 'one way'. There are many different ways to arrive at the same destination. The trick is to find out which one is the most enjoyable – and easiest – for you. Gather up all your favourite ways of doing things and create a beautiful, bespoke creation which will lead you to your dreams.

Step up onto the private jet in your mind. Make in amazing in there! I'm not saying you have to want a private jet. I love living a simple, elegant, low-cost lifestyle, but I also love having these sexy images, like *a private jet mindset*. What is your inspiring image I wonder?

Your Financially Chic inspirational ideas:

Choose your new mindset. Try it on like you are browsing in a boutique and see how it fits. Feel *inspired* and *excited* at the prospect of change. This is the start of wonderful new things for you.

Be in a positive mindset. *Every little thing helps*. Don't think, 'Why do I even bother?', 'Typical, I never win' or 'It's just how things are'. Discard those worn-out, shabby thoughts and choose yourself some new ones!

Here are some of my favourite mantras or affirmations to start you off:

Money is on its way to me
I love learning how to handle my finances with ease
My financial life is within my control
I get to have it all!
I live a first-class life
Wealth drapes over me like a cashmere blanket
I love feeling rich in all ways
I love my life!

Chapter 4.

Put your own spin on cutting back

There are two ways in which you can change the direction you are heading in with money, and they are:

Make more money
Cut back

Of course you can look into making more money, and maybe there is a side hustle you'd like to research or perhaps you will start looking for a different job. But these likely won't lead to increased income in the short term.

Cutting back, however, is something you can do *today*, and even small changes can make a big difference. The trick though, is to make cutting back *feel good*. No-one wants to feel deprived, or like they're missing out on all the goodness that others seem to have.

What you want to do is *find the flavour that most motivates you*. Allow me to share ideas which motivate me personally (and when I say 'motivate', it's a soft motivation, more of an excitement really).

These are angles which appeal to me and make 'cutting back' seem fun, enjoyable, and sustainable:

- **'Vintage homemaker'**. The wholesome feeling of book characters such as in *Little Women* where they lived simple and frugal lives, but were cultured and happy. This makes me want to read books, potter around my home making things lovely, go for walks at the beach or our local parks, and enjoy the simple things in life.

- **'Paris girl'**. The mythical idealistic French Chic girl who owns only three makeup items and ten pieces of clothing yet always looks stylish. From this feeling I am inspired to enjoy a small wardrobe, clear out items that aren't adding to my happiness, and be that thrifty Paris-inspired girl who reads in the sunshine sipping her black coffee.

- **'Move in silence'**. The Dave Ramsey ethos is of 'living like no-one else today so you can live like no-one else tomorrow'. I love the thought of quietly building wealth, flying under the radar, and making good choices on a regular basis when it comes to money.

- **'Luxury lifestyle'**. This is about living above your means in a way that is the *opposite* of how it sounds – seeing how big and lush you can make life while spending as little as possible. Dressing chicly and going for a walk along the waterfront in the winter (free), instead of sitting at a restaurant on the waterfront dining (costly). Enjoying public parks and their beautiful plantings, and having a simple garden at home. Borrowing the newest books from the library. Looking after your clothes and accessories and keeping them pristine and new-looking.

- **'Using things up'**. This is probably my favourite. After all, I've already spent money on items I own so I may as well use them. Plus I find that in doing so I fall in love with them all over again. I use all my lovely body products and fragrances. I create 'new' 21-piece 'Fiona Fashion' capsule collections (as detailed in Chapter 5 of my book The Chic Closet). And I make delicious, creative meals using up the food in my fridge, freezer and pantry.

I love all of these angles, and mix them together to make 'my flavour' of inspiration. Or, maybe some days might require a pure dose of just one. On a weekend where I want to play around in my closet and come up with some new outfits, I might invite my French girl in with me and we work together tiding, organizing, and creating.

You can add new flavour into your rotation too. You might dream it up, or come across an inspiring idea in a book or social media post. Maybe you'll be having a great journalling session and find a whole new motivation. Add it into your mix!

The most fun thing for me, apart from coming up with what inspires me in the first place, is to give them enticing names, almost like brand names, as I have in my examples above. Sell 'cutting back' as *the best fun ever*. You'll be so busy enjoying yourself that you won't even miss spending money!

Your Financially Chic inspirational ideas:

- Find out **what makes cutting back exciting** to you. Look to movies you enjoy, favourite books, and Instagram accounts that talk about money in a way that rings your bell. Think about times in your life when you found it easier to spend less and remember who you followed for inspiration then.

- Use **reverse motivation** if this is a better fit. Watch series like 'How to Get Rich' with Ramit Sethi on Netflix, and you will find yourself screaming in frustration at the screen with how unwise people can be with money. Then swear to yourself that *you* will never be that dumb!

- **Change your identity** from being a *spender* to someone who is *savvy and intentional* with their money, and who finds it *easy to accumulate wealth*. This might be a big step to begin with, so find a first small step to get you going in the right direction. An example might be tracking your bank accounts once a week, tallying up spending, and seeing if you can make a little goal for yourself such as a set amount of 'fun money' for the week.

Chapter 5.

Cut out 'everything'
and see what you miss

There is something deliciously empowering about taking back the reins of your spending. Set aside a little time to identify everything that is truly optional and consider cutting those things out, even if only temporarily. Some things you may miss, and others you won't at all. And, there will be expenditures that you find an even better replacement for which cost you much less. They may even be free!

Everyone's list of expenditures will look different of course, but it all starts in the same way – by looking through your bank account and credit card statements. You can do this online if you no longer have statements posted to you (which will be most of us).

You can get very detailed about it and download

statements to Excel where you can then re-order into categories such as groceries, fuel, streaming services, and internet shopping among others. Or you can simply scan down the columns, and note when you see something that isn't 100% necessary for survival.

I did this for our household a few months back. In doing so, I identified the following:

- **Our weekly cleaner**. Cleaning has always been my biggest stressor, and it made me so happy to have a team of two people come in each Monday and professionally clean our home while my husband was at work and I wrote my books. But since my husband's redundancy we decided to do the cleaning ourselves, with him doing the heavy jobs and me doing the lighter jobs. I have a lower back injury from twenty years ago that is exacerbated by vacuuming and mopping (it's all the twisting!) so I change the bed, clean the kitchen, and dust and primp while my husband vacuums and mops, and does the bathrooms and toilets. ***Savings: $125 per week***

- **One streaming service**. We decided which streaming service we'd miss the least and cancelled it. We still have a couple of others, but if we really needed to, we could cancel all of them and watch the DVDs we already own, and our free local television-on-demand channel with advertisements. ***Savings: $16 per month***

- **My monthly pedicure**. I have been getting a regular pedicure for a few years now (mostly just in the summer, but sometimes in winter too). I loved the pampering, loved that my nails were shaped perfectly, and loved the cheery red polish, but right now I can do my own pedicures. ***Savings: $50 per month***

- **My reflexology appointment**. I found a lovely lady who practices reflexology at her home studio, and I loved my monthly appointment. It felt like the best foot massage ever and I'd float out of there. I'm sure it had health benefits too because I felt so good afterwards (she said reflexology balances out hormones among other things), plus it was a blissful half-hour. But, our household's stability comes first. ***Savings: $40 per month***

- **My hair cut and colour**. Finally, my hair appointment every 10-12 weeks where I'd get foils, and a cut and blow-wave. Highlights and lowlights would blend in my dark blonde roots, grey hairs, and previously highlighted hair. I found a treatment that washes in and makes my grey hair look blonder, plus the darker roots not so obvious. I cancelled my next appointment to see how long I could hold out, perhaps going a few times a year instead of every 2-3 months. So far so good, and I found a lightening spray which softens my root colour too. ***Savings: $200-$250 each time***

~~

It has been a number of months since we made these changes, and here's what the current situation is.

Cleaning

We are still doing our own cleaning and I'm really enjoying getting reacquainted with my home again. We spend two hours every Monday morning resetting our home for the week and it feels just as good as if someone else has done it. We both wear our AirPods and do our jobs while listening to something interesting. ***Expenditure: $0***

Streaming Service

We have not gone back to our cancelled service, but my husband did buy a one-month Sky pass with a discount code to watch the Olympics. He is such a sports enthusiast, and since he is off work and it's winter here, why not have an indulgent time of it? It's still cheap entertainment. ***Expenditure: $40***

Pedicure
I did miss this, so I have had one pedicure so far! Crazily enough, the day I decided to book an appointment I received a 'We miss you!' email with a 10% discount code. ***Expenditure: $45***

Reflexology
Even though I really enjoyed this, I have not missed it like my pedicure, so I have not rebooked so far. And I know it's not the same therapeutically, but I massage my feet with thick body cream every night before bed. I have also conned my husband into giving me foot massages sometimes when we watch television together (lucky him!), so I'm still getting a little bit of pampering in. ***Expenditure: $0***

Haircut and colour
I have not missed this at all, especially since trying the John Freida lightening spray which blended my roots beautifully. I haven't needed a trim yet, but when I do I can simply comb my just-washed hair into a low ponytail and snip off the ends. I used to do this when we were saving for the deposit on our first home and it worked perfectly. Long hair is easy like that! ***Expenditure: $19***

As you can see, the savings have added up overall, even though we did have a few expenditures. We are $630 up, so far, and if we had no expenditures, we would be $730 up, every month! That's a lot to have as a recurring 'income', and it's tax-free too, because all these expenses were paid for with after-tax income.

I hope this chapter has inspired you to go through your recent expenditures and note down everything that you might call optional. Then, cut them all out and see what you miss. Maybe you will find significant savings like I did, or more, or less.

And as for upgrades, I actually prefer my new hair colour more, so it may be a long time before I go back to the hairdresser!

Your Financially Chic inspirational ideas:

- **Try this tip for yourself**. Scroll through the banking app on your phone and make a list of 'nice to have' spending as opposed to 'necessary' spending. Or you can print off a bank statement and cross out rent or mortgage, utilities and other necessities and then see what is left, if this works better for you.

- **Be brave and cancel future appointments**, and go online to take memberships and subscriptions off auto-renew. You can always go back to them later if you miss them.

- **Look for less expensive or preferably free ways** to get the same results. Sometimes you might consider the savings not worth worrying about, but every little cent adds up. This is how rich people often operate – they consider every expenditure no matter how small. Many wealthy people are *not* splashing the cash at every opportunity. That's for the ultra-rich, and broke people. None of us probably fit into the ultra-rich category (billionaire anybody?) and we definitely don't want to be in the broke category, so make like a rich person and be thoughtful of your spending.

Chapter 6.

Create money goals that inspire you

Can I just ask you, *Why are you reading this book? What drew you to it and what outcomes are you hoping for?*

Answer these questions for yourself, and as you do so, ponder your financial goals too. Ask yourself *what you want* (and *why*) and write everything down very clearly.

My question to you is:

What are your goals when it comes to your money and your finances?

Some examples of 'what' and 'why' could be:

- *I want to pay off my mortgage early – so I can be debt-free by the time I am 60 and have a happy retirement with no money worries.*

- *I want to clear my credit card once and for all and then pay it off each month when I use it – so I no longer have this heavy weight hanging over my head.*

- *I want to always have $2,000 in an account for unforeseen circumstances – so I have peace-of-mind that I can take care of things.*

- *I want to save for a family vacation – so we can have a relaxing and fun holiday, with no financial hangover.*

- *I want to save up to update our kitchen and pay for it in cash – so we can enjoy our beautiful new kitchen, and it's paid for in advance.*

- *I want to have funds saved for a new car before my old one needs replacing – so I can relax and not worry about my car breaking down and needing costly repairs.*

Whichever goal you choose for yourself, keep it top of mind. If you have more than one financial goal, prioritize which one you are going to work on first.

Write down your main goal in plain but enticing words and keep it in the front of your paper planner, pinned to your fridge, or as a reminder on your phone that pings up each morning to set you up for your day.

If you are more of a visual person, make or find a pretty vision board on Pinterest and set it as the screen saver on your phone or computer.

Our next financial goal is to give our kitchen a facelift and to do so with money saved rather than borrowing any. We won't redesign it completely in order to keep costs down, but new cabinet doors, benchtop, sink and taps, fridge/freezer, oven and cooktop, and flooring will definitely cost a bit.

We had decided to do it within the next year or two, to give ourselves time to save up. Of course, this goal is temporarily on hold until our finances are more plentiful, but we still know it's going to happen.

In the meantime I can pin or tear out beautiful kitchen images for ideas, and also to keep the dream alive in my mind. It's fun to think about, and we can quiz people who are having their kitchen updated (my sister and her husband currently) to gather useful information as well.

A bonus of the inspiring 'carrot' of our kitchen update, is that I won't fritter away money on home décor or anything that will take me further away from my goal. $20 here and $50 there soon adds up. Amounts like this are so easy to spend on cute items. They don't really feel like they could have any kind of negative financial impact, but they do!

Keep your goals in front of you

The more you remember your goals, the more likely it is you will achieve them. Reminding yourself often will help you keep on going – you are literally keeping the dream alive. Be sure to articulate your goals clearly and regularly to yourself, and to your other half as well. I love to say things like, 'Imagine if we...', 'Wouldn't it be amazing if...' or, 'Can't you see how beautiful our new kitchen is going to look?'

Just for fun, create a dreamy wishlist of your biggest goals and then make plans on how they could happen. Don't be defeatist and don't give up. If you never give up *you will eventually get there*, even if it seems like a big hill to climb.

Remember that cheesy 1980s motivational poster quote:

'Winners never quit, and quitters never win.'

You my friend, are a winner! And you never quit!

Your Financially Chic inspirational ideas:

- Sit quietly with a notebook and **consider your current money picture**.

  What are the facts?
  And, what would you rather the facts be?
  These are your goals.

- If you have more than one goal, which one would make **the greatest difference to your peace and happiness**, and relieve stress the quickest? *Choose that one.*

- Now that you know, you can **start making plans**. I promise they will be fun plans that will bring you joy and serenity. You can do it! Others have, so why not you. I've done it myself, so let me be your biggest cheerleader, and your guide as well. I am here for you!

Chapter 7.

Winning at the grocery store

I'm not going to pretend that I've ever really struggled to pay my grocery bill. I have never had to put necessary items back because I don't have the budget to cover them. I know this is a reality for many. But, like most people, I find it very concerning to see grocery prices go up, sometimes by the week. And remember how that same, normal, non-luxury item was half the price a year ago.

You might wonder when it's going to stop and then you see other categories increase as well, such as fuel or electricity, and you see that these will impact food prices yet again. It's hard to see café foods go up in price when you used to enjoy lunch out every once in a while, but you know the owners are hardly price gouging. They are probably barely keeping their heads above water. It's the same with retail stores. And the next week when you go past, you see their closing down signs in the window.

It's actually really disheartening. I can't bear the thought of people hurting, financially, emotionally and mentally. The area where I live has a population of around 165,000 and I know a lot of people are doing it tough. And even though our own household was able to handle my husband's job loss due to our decades-long thrifty ways, we are still looking for any way to cut back that we possibly can.

Enter the weekly supermarket shop. Groceries are one of the biggest weekly amounts we will spend aside from housing, fuel and utilities. And unlike other categories such as clothing, cosmetics, hobbies, books and toys, we can't just have a no-spend on groceries. We still need to eat. We still need toilet paper. And we still need shampoo to wash our hair. And we can't just stop feeding our pets!

Here are twenty ways in which I maximize the value I receive from my grocery spend. Not all of them will apply to you but some may. And, you might get new ideas to try which are sparked off from something on this list.

1. I look at what we already have in our fridge, freezer and pantry. Instead of simply topping up the cupboards, I make plans for meals to use the items I've already paid for (because food doesn't improve with age like wine does). It's like 'Shop your closet' but '**shop your kitchen**'!

2. I don't let leftovers and fresh produce go to waste. We make these into a lunch or dinner. We **prioritize using up items in our fridge** so that we get to use them before they are spoiled. Throwing food away is no different to throwing money away.

3. **I grocery shop once-a-week** on a Monday. This gives us a nice reset for the week with fresh groceries and a full fridge. I tried fortnightly but didn't like filling a huge trolley and trying to think what we'd need for the next two weeks. It was too stressful, so I went back to every Monday and it works perfectly for me. I only need to think about what I need for the next seven days.

4. We **cut our portion sizes**. This is both thrifty *and* healthy. Win/win! Meat and vegetables are stretched out, so we buy less. Instead of two glasses of wine each, we'd have one, and a bottle of wine would last a number of evenings instead of just one or two.

5. **I don't buy as many (or any) snack foods** – if they're not there I can't eat them. We always have cheese and crackers, and dark chocolate, so there is something there if I really want it, but these are not as tempting for me as potato chips and ice cream are.

6. **We cut our three dogs portion sizes** too! None of them are in danger of starving, and we had already been told that one of them is quite the solid size, so we trimmed down their breakfast and dinner, and they have a half-size lunch biscuit.

7. We also **stopped buying expensive dog treats** and they get a small dog biscuit as a treat instead. They like treats after dinner, but funnily enough they are not as keen on a dog biscuit as a Duck Tender! And, I think dog biscuits are healthier for them than treats, because I have heard that treats aren't considered 'food' and therefore not subject to the same food standards even though they are ingested, which I think is crazy.

8. **As soon as I open something** such as toothpaste or dental floss, it goes on the shopping list straight away. We won't need it in a while, which is perfect for me to check the price each trip and replace when it's on special. These days special prices are higher than the normal prices used to be, so it doesn't feel like much of a win, but it's still better than paying the new higher normal price.

9. At our supermarket, **when you spend $200 you get a free barista coffee**. Now, it's not difficult to spend $200 even on basic necessities these days so it's not like I'm spending extra money just to get a $5 coffee. But it is a fun game for me each week to spend as close to $200 as possible. Some weeks my bill might be $200.35 or similar! I use one of those trolley scanners, which I love for checking the prices of too, and this helps me keep a running total. I buy the must-haves for the week, and go through my list cherry-picking what I will also get. If something is on special I'll get it, but if it's not and we don't need it this week, I'll leave it for next week's shopping list. This might be more of a bother for you than it's worth, but for me I love the economics of it. And I'm only ever in the supermarket for 30-45 minutes at the most so it doesn't take me hours.

10. I **choose the cheapest supermarket** (*Pak N Save* here in New Zealand), and I go to the nicest of the three of this brand in our area. Luckily it's the closest to me. The trade-off is that there isn't a huge selection. If there is something specific that I need from a different supermarket, I'll call in there on the way home or at another time when I'm out. It's rare that I would need to do this though.

11. **I use an app on my phone called 'Grocer'.** It's just for New Zealand supermarkets I believe, but you may have something similar in your country. It lets me load in all the different brands and locations of the supermarkets near me, and I can compare prices on a particular product. I wouldn't make a special trip and use petrol in doing so, but if something is significantly cheaper at a different supermarket I'll get it when I'm out on an errands trip later in the week.

12. **Check stores for their own apps** too. One of the supermarket brands here (Woolworths) has a Rewards app, which I only use if it's extra good or we need something from there. I don't shop there as often as it is now one of our more expensive supermarkets, but when I work the Rewards well I can receive a $15 grocery voucher without too much effort or expenditure.

13. **I always check my receipt** before I leave the store. If you have been overcharged or charged for two items and only have one, it's far easier to get a refund for that because customer services is right there. In addition, one of our supermarket brands has a policy that you get your money back and the item for free if you are overcharged which is well worth taking advantage of.

14. I **check use-by dates** at the supermarket. Some stores are not good at rotating their stock, so get into the habit of checking, and choosing the latest date. Even if you plan on using the item in short time it's still nice to have the freshest one.

15. We **track pricing on high-value items** so we know when a special price is good. Meat is one example. The cuts we like such as skinless chicken thigh fillets are expensive so we buy one pack or skip that week. And, when they are on a super-special we might buy half-a-dozen packs and put all but one in the freezer so we won't need to buy it for a while.

16. We **buy commodity items on price**, such as butter or raw nuts. This is assuming I am happy with the country of origin. I always buy New Zealand produce as a preference. There is less of a carbon footprint, it's probably fresher, and I like to support my own country's economy.

17. Buy **fresh fruit and vegetables on special** and base your week's meals around these. Just like fancy chefs go to the markets each morning and choose what is freshest and the best value (both of which means that produce is in season and is therefore fresh and flavourful)!

18. **Don't assume a larger pack is better value**. Check the 'per gram' or 'per ounce' price if it's supplied on the price label, or do a quick calculation. Sometimes the smaller pack is less expensive per unit, especially if that size is on special and the larger size isn't.

19. **Don't overbuy perishables** even if they're cheap. Throwing out food is not saving money! At the moment vegetables are extremely inexpensive. A giant whole celery has been 99c the past few weeks, when we'd pay $3-$5 normally. But we already had a good amount left from our last week's shopping so we bypassed that special. It hurts to not partake in a bargain, but it hurts more to throw food away because you haven't used it soon enough.

20. **Store your fresh food well** when you get home. I have read that bagged salads are the most thrown out fresh produce item and I can believe it. Mesclun salad or fresh spinach can go slimy very quickly. It's enough to make you gag! I have a square food storage container that I line with a couple of paper towels, and tip the salad leaves in there while I am unpacking my groceries. The paper towels absorb excess moisture *and* keep the leaves fresh. Our bagged salads last as long as we need them to, at least a week. With broccoli I store it in a plastic bag, and reverse the bag every day or two, or

whenever I get it out to use some. I turn the bag inside out, shake the water drops into the sink, and put the broccoli back into the dry inside-out bag. This helps keep broccoli nicer for longer. Cauliflower really benefits from being wrapped in a paper towel then placed in a plastic bag.

As you can see from my examples, there are many different ways in which to make your grocery dollars go further and to minimize food waste too. And there will be a ton more if you search online.

How far you go is up to you, taking into account the amount of energy, time and patience you have for this category. But if you use even the easiest, most basic tips, you should be able to effortlessly trim money from your grocery bill. And money saved like this is just about free money. Free, tax-paid money. Who would say no to that!

Your Financially Chic inspirational ideas:

- **Decide on a schedule** for your grocery purchasing if you don't already have one. If possible, choose one day a week, or perhaps you will go every two weeks on your payday. Train yourself not to 'pop in for one or two things' in between times. Not only will you save a lot of time, but you will save a lot of money on impulse purchases. If you need a certain ingredient, improvise. Make do with what you have. And write items on your shopping list as you run out of them.

- Try to **get in and out of the supermarket as quickly as possible**. You don't need to jog around the shop, but be efficient, read from your list, and don't be tempted by the new lotion scents, potato chip special offers, or all the new herbal teas. It feels boring at the time to 'only get what you need' and have no snack options at home, but by the end of the week when you've saved money and haven't snacked as much, you will be very happy with yourself.

- **Make it a pleasant outing for yourself**. As I mentioned, I get a free coffee most weeks and I really look forward to it. Being free makes it taste that much better! I also have a good audiobook cued up to play driving there and back, plus I dress in a cute but practical outfit, wear nice daytime makeup, stud earrings, and style my hair. One week I had let my hair air-dry the day before grocery day, and it was in a bit of a frizz when I woke up, I must admit. But I smoothed it out with my blow-dryer, put on a fine faux tortoiseshell headband, and decided to tuck the length into a French pleat (French twist) style. While I was waiting for my free coffee, a lady who was just about to order said to me how much she loved my 'glam' hairstyle. That just showed me it doesn't take much effort to go from frizz to glam! And, that it's worth the effort, because I floated around the supermarket after that lovely comment!

Chapter 8.

Create your five-star hotel experience

Just because you've decided to make some changes and might not be able to eat out as much, go on vacation, or buy what you like doesn't mean you shouldn't live the five-star life. Really, this is the time you *should* be upgrading your experience. Anchor it in your mind that getting better with your money and building wealth is an *easy, fun, and relaxing way to spend your time.*

The key to living well with less is to make it an enjoyable practice. To have it be something you look forward to as well as feel empowered by. Shift yourself from gritting your teeth and putting up with it, to embracing this as *your era of rejuvenation and pleasure.*

Let this be a time when you get to use your creativity and find new ways of living. We can all get into ruts, but don't stay in one. Don't fight to stay in your rut! There are other things out there too!

Please allow me to share with you my favourite ways in which to *live a five-star life on a one-star budget*.

Start with a luxurious morning

What would you normally do if you had the chance to stay at a gorgeous five-star hotel? Probably have a little bit of a sleep-in, relax in bed with a coffee, and take a leisurely shower before getting ready to head downstairs to the restaurant for breakfast. Then, take a sight-seeing walk around the area in which you are staying.

Why not do this at home too? Maybe not on a workday, but on the weekend let yourself sleep in. Make your coffee and bring it back to bed instead of getting up straight away. Read a book or the weekend papers. Journal a little inspiration for yourself.

And the night before, have ingredients in your fridge for a hotel-style breakfast. Maybe you'll have sliced fruit and yoghurt, or scrambled eggs and sausage. With freshly brewed coffee of course!

Bespoke amenities

Something I love about staying in a nice hotel are the thoughtful details: little bottles of water, high quality body products, and specialty teas and coffee.

I love to recreate these at home for myself too. Even though I refill the water bottle that sits on my desk, in my car, or by my bed, I also keep a small supply of bottled water in case I need to dash out quickly, or want an extra for the car on a hot day.

In the case of body products, I adore prettily scented handwash, body lotions and creams, fragrance mists, and perfume. Some of mine are expensive, but mostly they are not. The most important thing to me is how a product works as well as it's fragrance. Maybe you love florals, or deliciously gourmand scents. Or perhaps you enjoy clean and crisp. Whatever your preference, keep your five-star bathroom amenities clean and polished, refilled and ready to go.

When it comes to tea and coffee, I love having a hot beverage station set up in the kitchen. It just feels more special to have my supplies gathered on a little tray rather than stashed in the pantry. I prefer Starbucks capsules, and have a petite selection of teas. I like to use them up and replace with fresh rather than keeping a huge selection that sits there for ages. Commit to using up tea and coffee if you have an oversupply, then refresh your selection with the ones you like best.

Turn down your room

Something I love to do each night is turn down our bedroom. It's winter in New Zealand as I write this, so it gets dark quite early – around 5pm. As soon as the sun disappears, I close the curtains in our bedroom to keep the heat in.

At the same time I take the big European pillows from our bed, as well as the small velvet pillow which sits in front. I place them on the guest bed across the hall so that our room looks nice and spacious. Have you noticed that in a hotel the extra pillows disappear from your bed when your room is turned down? This is what I do for myself!

I know I could close the curtains when I go to bed at 9pm or 10pm, but it's so much nicer to come into our bedroom and have nothing extra to do beyond washing my face and brushing my teeth. And since I did the turndown so many hours before, it's almost like someone else did it for me. I don't put a chocolate on the pillow (wouldn't that be fun though?) but I do put my freshly refilled water bottle by the bed.

During turndown, you might also take a quick minute to put away any folded washing, your handbag, and laundry in the hamper. It's a nice reset to prepare you for a good night's sleep.

~~

These are just a few ways in which to bring that five-star hotel feeling to your home. Recall or imagine for yourself what could be a fun five-star experience you'd like to partake in? Even if just on the weekends or for a special treat?

Your Financially Chic inspirational ideas:

- Put **a small collection of magazines or a couple of coffee table books** out, and rotate them weekly (maybe they even come from the public library). Sit down with a coffee and browse through them as if you are relaxing in a five-star club lounge.

- **Create a 'check-in' when you get home** just like checking into a hotel – maybe after work? Your handbag is emptied out and put away. You change your clothes and relax for a bit before cooking dinner. You can enjoy a refreshing beverage at this time too.

- Dedicate a whole journalling session and brainstorm all the ways in which you can **create a five-star hotel experience in your life** as it is right now, on exactly the same income.

Chapter 9.

Feel richer with the
'upside down' method

Whether you love the Law of Attraction and live your life by it, or are 100% a practical person, there is something so refreshing and invigorating about letting go of items that are worn out, make you feel depressed just looking at them, or have a not-great memory attached, even if small.

You might wonder, 'Well why would I have those things in my house, I'm not an idiot', and I know you aren't! Just like I know I'm not an idiot, but these things can just creep into your house while you are asleep and set up residence without you even noticing.

Maybe because it is by degrees – your underwear isn't going to start out pristine and brand-new one day and be stretched out and tired looking the next.

It's a hard line to judge for some of us who are used to getting the most from every purchase. I am definitely one of those people.

I don't find it difficult to throw out a chipped glass, torn or stained piece of clothing (that cannot be mended or cleaned), or something that is clearly past its best. But I do find it hard to judge the pristine-ness.

The best way to see it with fresh eyes is to *do one category at a time*, which I prefer simply so I don't procrastinate in tidying up my closet. *'It's such a big job! I'll wait until I have one whole day to organise my clothes!'* Two months later I'm still talking about my messy closet...

Category by category, combined with *the 'upside down' method*, is how I win the game, and you can too. Let's say you want go through your sleepwear and loungewear. You know there are some worn-out items in there but you've managed to ignore them for a while. You just pick around them and wear what you prefer!

The 'Upside Down' method

I find it hard to reach into my drawer and pull out the things I don't want. What works far better for me is to tip everything out onto my bed, one drawer at a time.

When you do this, you will immediately have an empty drawer – a clean space to work with. Then, go through the items on your bed and choose your favourites and newests first. Refold them, enjoying how pretty they are, how much you love the colours, and how new they look! Then place them in your empty drawer and go through the pile again.

As you come across items that look past their best, or you simply dislike wearing them for whatever reason (the fabric isn't soft enough, or they've always had a dowdy vibe in colour or style), either cut them up for cleaning rags if the fabric is appropriate, throw them out, or put them in a donation pile if they're in good condition. Even better, go and get a shopping bag and put the donation pile directly in there – it's one less barrier to actually donating these items.

You may find you haven't gotten rid of that much, maybe only a handful of items, or perhaps none at all if this category was only recently organized. But what you will find is that you have become reacquainted with what you own, you love everything because you have only kept the best, and your happiness in this category is increased as a result!

I promise you, the next day when you open the drawer to choose something, you will get a happy thrill when you see that everything is pleasing to your eye, you don't have to fossick around past the items you don't like, and the drawer closes easily too!

You can use the *upside down* method anywhere:

On your bookshelf. Remove one whole category of books whether it's cookbooks, your beloved collection of 'living well' books, non-fiction, or self-help. Wipe the shelf down quickly, and then start putting back your favourites. If some seem dull or dreary, the feel of the book doesn't excite you, or the font is too small or too light, put them in a donation box. *Gaze in wonder at your new, exciting bookshelf.*

In your kitchen. Let's say you choose glasses as your category. Take them all out onto the counter, wipe that shelf down, and start putting the glasses back neatly, starting with the ones you love the most. As you get down to orphans and glasses that you never use, pop them into a donation box and again, *gaze in wonder at your lovely glasses shelf.*

Can you see a theme here? And it's not that these items are necessarily worn out, but if they give you a feeling of 'Urgh, I should read that but I don't want to', or 'I used to use these glasses a lot, but there's only one left now and actually, it's looking a little cloudy', they don't belong in your home.

It seems counterintuitive to get rid of stuff when you are looking to feel more abundant, but this is exactly what will happen. When you keep only the nicest and newest of any category, and remove anything that brings you down, you will feel 'richer'.

Everything you have kept will seem brand new! Try it in one category, and then tell me how you feel. I promise, you will feel amazing. You will have a little zing of excitement down your legs, in a good way!

Your Financially Chic inspirational ideas:

- **Note the categories** that immediately come to mind for you.

- Choose one and **start on it straight away** (one category often takes only 15-30 minutes, if that).

- **Enjoy the wonderful feeling of being in action**. Donate or throw out any removed items as soon as you can. Closing the loop is where the real magic happens.

Chapter 10.

Cultivate your rich lady lifestyle

Even if you are facing restriction in your budget and making the necessary cuts, whether extreme or just a little bit, there is no need to feel poor or broke. To inspire yourself as you get back on track, choose for yourself that you are living *your rich lady lifestyle*.

In your rich lady life, the sun is always shining and people treat you like a *celebrity*. You dress well every day, appropriate to what you are doing. You feel upbeat, uplifted, and upmarket. All the ups!

You **grocery shop as if you live in high society**, choosing fresh, luscious fruits, and water-rich crispy vegetables. You turn your nose up at processed snack foods because they will not feel well in your body and simply put, they are not good enough for you.

You **pamper yourself** using all the products you already own – creamy body lotion, painting your nails, wearing makeup, and your nicest perfume. You apply face masks every week, either store-bought or natural recipes found online.

You **take self-care to the extreme** and dine like a wealthy lady, with fresh, delicious foods, and chilled sparkling water. You love nothing better than to curl up in bed at night with a good book. You sleep deeply and well by valuing sleep hygiene, and wake up refreshed and vibrant each morning. You create a healthy glow by going for outdoor walks, and stretching luxuriously whenever you can.

You **streamline your closet** and keep only your nicest and newest items. Anything that makes you feel frumpy or poor goes – not just to another closet, but out of the house. You wear the scarves and costume jewellery you have collected. You dress for your day. You enjoy looking after your clothes and hanging them back up again once they have been washed and ironed.

You **enjoy the sun** outside, or **feel cozy inside** if it's raining. You make life wonderful for yourself by putting together a nice lunch to take to work, and bringing a good book to read on your break.

You pride yourself on **your luxurious mindset** and journal beautiful inspiration each morning. You read and absorb the books on your shelves at home. You create beauty, even if just in tiny ways, everywhere you go. You maintain high standards in all areas of your life; this includes what you consume, with food and drink, and media too.

You are grateful for every day, and if you ever feel that life is 'boring', you give yourself a little pep talk and point out everything that is glorious – *there is so much*. It's worth it to you to be the Pollyanna of your life because it helps you appreciate all your riches, and makes you feel happier too.

You are in **control of your emotions** and **elegantly self-possessed**. You are on time, unhurried, and relaxed. You cultivate the freedom of time, firstly in your mind, and this filters out into your world.

You have a quiet demeanour, and when you speak (which is rare), people lean in to listen. **You have mystique** and don't share every little detail of your life. You are above petty things too, refusing to gossip (unless it's 'good gossip' where you talk others up), and no longer enjoy dramatic scenes (unless they are in a fabulous movie), sarcasm or self-deprecating humour.

There is no downside to cultivating your rich lady lifestyle. All that will happen is that you will feel more *abundant, resourceful, positive,* and *radiant.* Life is good, very good, regardless of trimmed financial circumstances. You will always be okay!

No-one even has to know that you have taken on this new, shinier persona. You can keep her tucked into your secret garden. Then, one day they will notice, 'Something is different about you, what is it?' You can give them a small shrug and a smile and say, 'I don't know, I've just been feeling good lately'.

Your Financially Chic inspirational ideas:

- **Ponder the flavour of *your* rich lady lifestyle**. Does she go out more or stay in? Is she private or social? What does she enjoy wearing? What colours, fabrics, styles? Does she eat differently to you? What does she choose as a hot or cold beverage? Where does she get her inspiration from? What does she enjoy reading?

- **Look around your home and see just how much you have already**. Books to read, candles to light, fragrances to enjoy, a green view from your bedroom window. Give each room a good tidy and clean, and declutter a few items too. See how this freshens everything up and makes the room look *fresher* and *newer*.

- **Look at how you live through the eyes of someone less fortunate**. You really do have it all! There is so much goodness – so much *richness* – in your life. Sure you've had a temporary setback, and that's all it is, temporary. Most situations are. But you know you will come through it stronger and happier, because you always do.

Chapter 11.
Make the most of your current prosperity

Many of us have *a lot* in our homes, as evidenced by all the decluttering advice around – including a book by me called '100 Ways to Declutter Your Home'! We simply have too much. When you think about it, isn't right now *the perfect time* to use what you have? To make the most of the items you already own?

I am sure if you took a moment to walk around your house, peeking into cupboards and on shelves, you would find a *bounty* of goodness. What is it that *you* have an abundance of?

Food and drink?
Clothing, hobbies, or beauty products?
Sporting or camping equipment?
Children's toys?

Tech items?
Cleaning supplies even?

Imagine getting a calculator and adding up the purchase of everything you already own. None of us will ever do this, I know, but it would be a lot! Many thousands if not tens of thousands at a guess.

Identifying what we have is the first way we can shift our thinking from lack and stress to a feeling of plentiful richness.

And the second way is to **use what we have**.

Instead of the default action being 'let's buy more', why not switch it to 'let's enjoy what we've already got'.

Make it a fun game to get *the most value* from items you've already paid for. Feel that lovely dopamine hit when you put a new outfit together from pieces already in your closet, or use the last drop of fragrance that you've had at the back of your bathroom cupboard and can now recycle the bottle.

'Using things up' is a natural way to declutter your home too, and you may become hooked on it! It's certainly one of *my* favourite things to do. I get a real high from making a meal incorporating a jar that has been hanging around in the fridge door (as long as it's within the expiration date of course). It's just so satisfying!

I also love cutting open a body lotion tube and

scraping the last of the product out with my finger. Using 'the free part' really does give me a thrill.

Clothing and footwear

What about with your apparel though? You don't really 'use up' clothes, not fully, but you can make them more appealing and fresh to your eyes. Iron them perfectly. Shave those little friction bobbles off a sweater and make it look new again. Sticky roller any fluff or pet fur off clothes. Reorganise your closet and tidy everything up. As you do all these things remember why you bought that item and recall the excitement at the time of purchase.

'Shop your closet' by pre-making an outfit complete with accessories. Hang it up so you can enjoy the creative process you've just been through, and you'll also be happy the next day when you have a lovely outfit ready to wear!

Food and drink

In lean times you will naturally want to cut back on grocery spending. Make it a fun game by creating meals using ingredients you have already. Decide that this is the time to 'eat your freezer' and use up every last bit of fresh food in your fridge.

If you don't have an ingredient, make do rather than driving to the supermarket. Have frozen peas instead of fresh broccoli. If you don't have any coleslaw, make a 'salad' of tomatoes dressed in olive oil and a crunch of salt and pepper over top. If you are stuck for a substitution, search online for 'cooking substitute for X' and you will find loads of helpful (and sometimes surprisingly excellent) ideas.

Cleaning supplies

If you're like me, you will have extra cleaning supplies that never seem to get used up. As with pantry items, extras can get pushed to the back while newer products are used. Make it your mission to use up your cleaning supplies. They aren't cheap after all.

And the bonus is that your home will never look better! I'm thinking of furniture polish that I use occasionally, but I mostly spray-and-wipe my dining table. But I know that when I use the polish, my vintage timber dining table gleams. What am I waiting for, the polish to dry out and become all cracked so it's unusable?

Books and entertainment

I'm sure you have books and DVDs at home that you've never even opened. I have! Designate a movie night and watch those old DVDs if you've cut down on streaming services for a while. And, make it your mission to read all the books you own.

At the moment, I am making it a goal to read the books on my bookshelf as much for the shelf space as anything. Non-fiction favourites I keep because they are books I love and will reference often such as my French Chic-genre titles. But novels I have been donating once I've read them, apart from a couple of favourites which I like to re-read every so often.

In doing this, I've found one novel that I couldn't get into, so that went into my donation bag unread. And it was the same with a London biography which had a bookmark half-way through it *from before I knew my husband* (we met in 2003)!

I recalled really enjoying the first half so decided this would be the next book I picked up. It did *not* hold my interest, and flicking forward could see it never would, so that was also donated without finishing.

Obviously I'd received the value from this book two decades ago yet I have moved house multiple times with it since. This made me even more determined to read through my bookshelf and clean it up. I don't want to move in the future (whenever that might be) lugging books I have no interest in!

If you've already read all your books, go to the library for books and audiobooks. Request that they order in your favourites – you can do this with mine too! You can request audiobooks and paperbacks of my books to be ordered in at your local library. I love to think of my books in libraries all around the world, being discovered by people and helping them feel happier!

Your personal favourites

This category will encompass those items you seem to have multiples of without even trying. Mine are candles, perfumes, and body products. I love pretty scents in both! But I can also enjoy what I have without buying any more for a while.

My husband is a wine enthusiast, and he loves picking up good quality wines at bargain prices. But since we are in a season of thrift, he has been buying far less and letting his cellar dwindle a little. This way, when there really is a well-priced special offer, he can buy a few bottles without guilt.

You know how you can 'coast' in a car, seeing how far you can travel without putting your foot on the gas? Why not coast for a while with your favourite indulgences too.

Your Financially Chic inspirational ideas:

- **Think about the categories you can't say no to**. This will be a natural place to start and I'm sure you will already be thinking about just how much you have in these categories already. Energetically cut off spending for now, delete bookmarks and unsubscribe from mailing lists. Then, enjoy what you have. I have found that when I do this, I really do fall in love all over again with items I've previously grown used to. Read positive online reviews if you need an extra push! I do this with perfumes I've become used to, and it makes them seem new to me.

- **Visit your kitchen and make an inventory list**. I do this when our freezer gets a bit full, but you could include your fridge and pantry also. Make yourself a little menu like a restaurant and put together fresh, frozen or pantry items to create delicious *free* meals.

- **Plan an afternoon where you put outfits together** in your closet, and even take photos of them for future reference. Channel someone you admire style-wise and let them be your muse while you organize and style.

Chapter 12.

Dream of your beautiful future

Imagine, just for a moment, that you were having five-million dollars deposited into your bank account in thirty days time. It's a done deal, and all you have to do is look forward to it.

Or perhaps you've just been notified that you got that job you applied for, and you start in two weeks. The salary is double what you received in your last job, your working hours are just twenty hours a week, and you will receive more in benefits than you ever have.

For me, a wonderful scenario is that one of my books has been picked up by someone influential who loved reading it, and is telling everyone on social media about my books and that they need to read them too. I would love being able to reach more people by a stroke of luck!

Let the dream marinate

Whatever scenario is most exciting for you, or perhaps an even better one has popped into your mind, take a minute to imagine how it would feel, and what you might do.

You wouldn't feel sad and scared about money being tight, because you already know plenty is on its way to you. Envisaging a bright daydream like this enables you to *act as if*, to feel positive about future offerings, and to be more pro-active and solution-focused instead of down in the dumps.

In my scenario I could feel like there's no point in writing my books because people are cutting back on discretionary spending. I could feel like I don't have anything new to say and I should just give up on my books and go and get a job somewhere. I don't really feel like that because I am always cultivating a positive mindset and inspiring myself to dream up material for my next book, so let's pretend I had writer's block and wasn't motivated.

But if I knew that someone incredibly famous was about to discover my books, do you think I'd have a pep in my step? Do you think I would show up on social media regularly, and be busy working on my newest book? You bet I would – it would be exciting to imagine!

What about you, having just gotten that job which pays twice as much and only working half the time? Would that get you out of that rut you've been in and put a happy smile on your face?

Imagine showing up at your current job with that future promise in mind. I can imagine you'd get ahead there even, with your cheerful attitude and can-do style. Customers would send in happy feedback and it would come to the attention of your manager. You may even be offered a promotion!

Or lets go back to the first scenario, you've been notified by your bank officially (and it's definitely not a scam!) that a cool five-million dollars will be deposited into your account in exactly thirty days' time. Just let that sink in for a moment. You're picturing your bank balances, your credit card, and your car loan. You're seeing your mortgage too perhaps.

All debit balances will be wiped, and you'll have a lot in your everyday account *and* your on-call savings account too.

What kind of a person do you think you'll be after this happens? Would you be worrying and fretting? No. But I don't think you'd be the kind to blow it all either. No, you'd feel confident, secure and safe. You'd know you were taken care of, for life if you want to be.

How to bring *acting as if* into your real life

I get that all these scenarios are imaginary though, so how do we draw them into our real life, since we don't have 100% control over any of these situations? In each of the examples I have outlined, they have the ability to change how we think and feel, how we act, and how we perceive ourselves.

Choosing your favourite and letting it be infused into your daily life brings out who you really are, your authentic likes, and how you want to live. Imagine waking up with five million dollars in the bank and asking yourself how you would ideally live.

What would you do for a job?
What would you do for fun?
How would you dress?
How would you act?
How would you live your life?
Are there things you would change from how you live now?

I would add to this the confidence piece. Would you feel more secure in who you wanted to be if you had a solid financial backing? The good news is that we can begin to create this for ourselves all by switching our mindset around.

We get ourselves into a better feeling state of mind by dreaming and *acting as if*, and this spurs us into helpful actions, inspired ideas, and being happily productive. Just thinking about my books possibly going viral makes me want to brainstorm new ideas for books, write more each day, and design beautiful covers for upcoming books. The possibility is exciting, and it spurs me on.

Thinking back to when I worked in a job and then our own retail business, I'd show up each day with a positive attitude. I'd look for extra jobs to do, and I would radiate helpfulness and good cheer to customers and colleagues alike. I'd whizz through my work, be a ray of sunshine, and probably enjoy my job more as well as creating more prosperity for myself.

And that's how we can create forward momentum for ourselves. We can pump ourselves up with possibility and it becomes a fun game, effortless too. Take a little time to dream today, and see what you come up with!

Your Financially Chic inspirational ideas:

- Do any of my three scenarios ring your bell? Or do you have a different one? Whatever you choose, take some time to **close your eyes and visualize it**, or open your journal and **brainstorm a list** of bullet points on how you would feel, what you might do, and the kind of person you imagine being. Let your fantasies flow, and don't hold back.

- While you're at it, why not try the five-million dollar exercise and see **what your dream life might look like**.

- With both of these exercises **enjoy the positive feelings, confidence, and ideas** you will receive. Go through your findings and pick out any real-life pieces that you can implement *today*. For example, maybe in your ideal life you relax with yoga for ten minutes before bed. Or go out for a nice lunch once a week. Or take time to read regularly. Are there components listed that you can bring into your real life today? Because that's what we are trying to do – lessen the distance between our ideal life and our current everyday life. It's actually not that hard to do, I promise you. You can feel freer and more joyful with new, little actions. And it all comes from your mindset!

Chapter 13.
Can you afford your lifestyle?

A big question to really get honest about is, 'Am I willing to put the time and effort in for the upkeep of the lifestyle I live?'

For me personally, I wouldn't want a huge mortgage and expensive lifestyle that is causing me massive stress. Nothing is worth my peace of mind.

If you have financial pressure right now but can see a way out, you may be happy to keep on going and just tweak a few things. But if you can't even see the light at the end of the tunnel you might want to choose a different path, and there's no shame in that. You may think people will judge you for downsizing when the common measure of success is a big fancy home and two late-model cars, but they're not the ones paying for it. *You are.*

There's a great saying that goes, 'Rich people stay rich by acting poor, and poor people stay poor by acting rich'. I think there is a lot of truth in that! I see people spending a lot more than I would on various purchases and experiences, and then once I get to know them I find out that actually, we may well be wealthier than they are. But it doesn't feel like we are, because they are the ones with the beautiful, expensive designer clothes, brand-new cars, and who travel lavishly and often.

I have actually been made fun of multiple times by someone we know because I am thoughtful with my money. 'Oh typical Fiona, she's always after a bargain'. Can you guess that this person and their family are perpetually in financial crisis and have been for decades? I somehow don't think things are going to change either.

What about you? Do you feel like you need to get honest about your financial situation? Do you feel stressed daily and wonder how you can keep on going?

Well, what if there were some out-of-the-box, possibly extreme ideas that could help you sail into more serene financial waters? Out of the choppy seas and into a safe and peaceful cove?

Would you consider **selling your home** and buying something smaller or moving elsewhere? This is not an option you can implement as quickly as other ideas in this book, but it might be a very important one.

If it's not a good time to sell, can you rent a

smaller home and rent out *your* house? Or would you consider renting a guest room to an out-of-town student or young worker? Look online to see what a room rents for in your area and consider if it would be worth the hassle to you. Maybe it can be something you'd decide to do for a year, and be willing to sacrifice the loss of privacy in order to pay off debt, or save for a family vacation.

If **buying a home** is beyond you right now, could you buy an apartment or a small unit and live in it? Then, when you can afford more, your first home could become the first property in your investment portfolio.

Or, if what you can afford is too small or impractical for your requirements (perhaps you can afford to buy in a different area but it's too far to commute), can you continue renting where you do, but buy a property to rent out to someone else?

These are all big decisions that you will want to take financial advice about, but it's an example of thinking outside the box and doing something that others might not be willing to do or haven't thought of.

What about **owning one car instead of two**, and sharing with your other half? Would that work for you? Perhaps it might if you have good public transport where you live, or if you work from home like I do. You would receive a lump sum of money that can go towards debt or a house deposit, plus you wouldn't have the associated costs such as car payments, insurance, registration, and maintenance. Or if you have a car that's on its last legs, maybe you just won't replace it.

Are there other **high-ticket items you could sell** and free up ongoing money such as a tropical fish tank, leisure boat, or other expensive hobby? A colleague we know told us he sold his expensive brand-new boat, paid off the loan with the proceeds, and considered that the time he'd owned it for was renting, not owning it. He loves fishing, it's his favourite thing ever, but he loved not having that high monthly payment, especially when his business started slowing due to the recession.

Consider everything, even the outrageously outlandish ideas. You never know, one of them might work for you. Or another idea could be sparked off showing you a perfect way to free up some cash and possibly even make you happier living a simpler life.

Forget what others might think about your choices. They are not the ones waking up at night wondering if they can ever afford to retire. Personally, nothing is worth financial stress. My highest priority is peace of mind. If you feel the same, have a think about what you could sell, downsize, or lessen the outgoings on. And at the same time, are there ways you can bring in more money?

Talk to your partner about it and let them know how stressed you are. The best conversations I've had with my husband Paul are when I've gone to him and said, 'This is really worrying me and I don't know what to do about it.' I always feel a million times better when I lay my heart bare and am open to his input.

If you are married or living with another person, you are in this together. You may be the keeper of the dream, but it's wonderful when you know you are both on the same page. One of the best quotes I've heard about partnerships is this one, by Antoine de Saint-Exupery, who said: 'Love is not just looking at each other; it's looking in the same direction.' I really love the thought of both of us looking in the same direction, building our life together.

Maybe you'd like a big change?

Have a think about your lifestyle, whether you can afford it easily, and also if you might prefer something different. It's not that common, but people do make complete life changes.

My brother chose to sell up his entire life and move overseas, to a country that is less expensive to live in, and that he has always loved visiting. He now lives a permanent 'on vacation' lifestyle of fitness, health and relaxation in Thailand. Of course this wouldn't suit everyone, I personally love living in New Zealand and would probably get terribly homesick. But just knowing there are options outside of the norm makes life interesting, don't you think!

Your Financially Chic inspirational ideas:

- **Audit your lifestyle expenses** as if you were a consultant employed to do a financial assessment. Walk around the house and look into closets, the garage, and kitchen cabinets and see if there are any bigger ticket items. The biggest of course being your home and vehicles and how much they are costing you each month.

- **Look into renting out a room,** or even your garage for parking if you live in the city. I have heard of commuters renting a private garage near their work in preference to paying parking building fees.

- I know this chapter might seem a little extreme, but it's the kind of people who think outside-the-box who are considered to 'always land on their feet' from an outsider's perspective. Become one of those people by **being willing to do the things others aren't willing to do**.

Chapter 14.

Journal your rich lady lifestyle into reality

To give your rich lady lifestyle in Chapter 10 even more of an inspired boost, take a little journalling session for yourself and dream up *all* the details. You might want to do this at home, in a café, or even a park. Make it comfortable and pleasurable, and be sure to have a delicious beverage by your side – maybe a flavoured sparkling water or café crème.

Pull out your notebook and allow yourself to indulge in your lifestyle aspirations. I decided for myself that I was going to create a 'soft lady lifestyle'. I imagined the luxurious, elegant apartment she would live in. Of course I have a husband and pets, but when I did this journaling I imagined it was just me living by myself in a beautiful, luxurious brand-new apartment. I didn't want to take into account the practicalities I'd have to consider so that I wouldn't feel constricted. I didn't want anything to break my flow!

The result was a list so delightful and inspiring to me, and amazingly, it could apply to my life right now. I re-read this list regularly and feel myself floating into that dreamy feeling of bliss you get sometimes. The kind of feeling when you are on vacation, lying by the pool in the sun. Or perhaps when everything is just perfect at a family gathering and you brim with satisfaction at all the laughter and fun happening around you. *That* kind of blissful feeling.

Imagine if a happy journalling session produced something that you could enjoy reading and dial up a feeling of delight on demand? Wouldn't that be wonderful?

Please allow me to share my soft lady apartment lifestyle with you, and maybe you'll be inspired to create a dreamy manifesto for yourself as well.

Fiona's soft lady lifestyle:

- She lives a feminine life.

- She moves slowly and intentionally.

- The colours surrounding her are soft, light, and airy: pale pinks, blush beige, creamy whites, with floral and gold accents.

- She surrounds herself with cozy touches such as soft textures, and flattering lighting - lamps, a luxurious throw, and perhaps a plush rug.

- Natural light is diffused throughout her home via white shutters or sheer curtains.

- On her coffee table are flowers, a candle, and display books.

- She has an elegant and simple kitchen, filled with healthy foods. There is plenty of free space in the cupboards and drawers. She only has the nicest of everything e.g. 4-6 new tea towels and they are replaced when worn.

- Her bed is beautifully appointed in thick, supple white linen. In the winter a cozy rug is folded at the foot of the bed.

- She has a streamlined array of fragrances and body products.

- She reads books, plays soft music, journals, and writes her books too.

- She earns a very good income and has investments. She is financially secure.

- She meets friends for lunch or coffee.

- She goes to see movies at the theatre by herself, or with others. She loves going to arthouse movies.

- She takes herself on long meandering walks around the neighbourhood and enjoys doing stretching, yoga and Pilates at home.

- Her home is peaceful, calm, fragrant, inspiring, uplifting, and supports her wellbeing.

- Her bathroom has the decor and atmosphere of a luxurious French perfumier spa retreat. Pristine white towels are changed out regularly.

- She rises early in the morning and retires early in the evening, enjoying a full eight hours of restful sleep.

- She loves the freedom of being fully in charge of her own space, time and schedule.

- She sees people on her own terms and recharges by spending time alone.

- She dines lightly and often has pre-prepared protein and vegetables.

- She makes herself snacky bistro boxes for lunch with such foods as fresh fruit, cheese, olives and pepper dews.

- She is confident enough to put forward her preferences and has long learned to be self-possessed while still being kind and soft.

- She marches to the beat of her own drum and follows her inner guidance in preference to trends, whether it be clothing, music, interior design, diet types or whatever trend or movement is in vogue.

- She stays informed and up-to-date but keeps news to a minimum. She would rather watch a movie or gentle television series, or read.

- She regularly maintains those categories which are important to her: her wardrobe is streamlined, organized and cared for. She keeps her car clean and serviced. Her handbag is immaculate, inside and out. Her financial records are in order. She takes care of her grooming (hairstyle, skincare and makeup, home manicures, self-tanning, epilation, and exfoliation). She loves doing all these things.

- She curates music for her mood (luxury hotel vibes, calming instrumental, classic jazz, female blues singers, and her Dior relaxing music playlist).

- She lights candles daily whether they are scented or not. She enjoys both.

- She is inspired by the styles of Lisa Vanderpump, Aerin Lauder, and Ralph Lauren.

I love the whole feeling of this list! Can you feel the peaceful abundance and ladylike details like I can? And the fun thing too, is when you journal a vision such as this for yourself, you can take on this persona today. I can certainly do a lot of the things on this list in my current home and situation. I don't have to wait for that mythical perfect 'one day' when I live in a luxury apartment.

And, when I do choose something to purchase, or we plan a change for our home (such as our kitchen revamp), it can lean towards my soft lady apartment lifestyle, right here at our practical, comfortable 25-year-old home in the country.

Something that came from this list that I've decided to do that is not my usual, is to go and see an arthouse movie when a film festival comes to town. My husband Paul is not a fan of subtitles, but I really enjoy the cultured feeling of watching a movie in French or another language. That's okay though, if he doesn't want to go, I can still go and enjoy myself!

Why is it such a big deal to go to a movie with others anyway? After all, we sit there watching it by ourselves. I guess you can discuss it afterwards, that's half the fun, but not having someone to go with wouldn't stand in my way, that's what I'm trying to say.

And details such as the white towels, we have white towels already that we use, so I already have this dialled in!

Feminine décor is something that really calls to me, but my husband also has to be comfortable living here. Somewhere I *could* go all out and make ultra-feminine and in my idealistic dreamy soft lady style, is my office where I write my books. It's a small room, triangular in shape, and it's the perfect space for me.

It looks out over our driveway and the road, which is nice because I like to know what's happening and see who is coming or going. When we first moved here I took one of our guest rooms as my office because it has a gorgeous view overlooking the apple orchard below us. But it felt like I was tucked away at the back and I found I much preferred to see the road, plus the front door is right by me. I feel more part of things.

With my office, I could definitely declutter a few of the more practical things or tuck them away out of sight, and bring the vision I have into reality right now. It's already soft and feminine with a white desk and creamy white walls, sheer light-filtering curtains and feminine prints on the wall, so only a little tweaking and prettifying is required.

If you do this exercise for yourself, you will find that you strip back all the things that don't belong and save only the very best and most elevated details for your idealistic life. It's fun to dream about, and even more fun to bring those dreamy details into reality!

Your *Financially Chic* inspirational ideas:

- Book some time out in your schedule, maybe an hour, to **dream and write in your notebook**. It doesn't have to be done in one session. Allow the ideas to come to you, and when you see something in a movie or book, jot those ideas down too. Include beautiful words that move you, colours, and music too. Intentionally seek out further inspiration to enhance your experience!

- Once you have a list that thrills you, like mine does for me, **re-read it often**. Fall to sleep dreaming of the possibilities and the vision. Pluck specifics out and include them in your current life; bring your idealistic lifestyle to your real life one beautiful detail at a time.

- If you have the budget for it, maybe you'll buy a few new things, but for me it's more fun to dream and then do **without spending anything at all**. It's more about what you are removing – editing if you like. Be the Editor-in-chief of your life!

Chapter 15.
Identify what you value

To feel good about making possibly unwelcome or uncomfortable changes such as cutting back your spending, it helps to *find your underlying principles*. Take a moment to think about what you value, and what inspires you. If someone asked you 'What is important to you in life?' or 'What would make your life feel happy and complete?', how would you respond?

When I ask these questions of myself, I get straight away what is important to me and how I'd like to spend time in my ideal life: For me it's all about:

- Living **a simple and elegant life** where I don't need to earn a ton of money simply because I don't lead an expensive lifestyle.

- Having **a stress-free life** (as much as possible), by not creating money worries for myself with how I spend.

- Making my money work hard for me by **being a savvy person** when it comes to buying anything I need.

- **Creating my own 'free entertainment'** by reading books, having friends around, or going for a Sunday stroll in a beautiful public area. Not everything has to be about spending money. In fact, I prefer free things to paid things. Why wouldn't I!

Reading through this list is highly motivating to me, and instead of feeling deprived if I don't buy anything, I feel *liberated*. Instead of spending my money, *I am giving it to myself instead*.

To take this exercise a step further, extract the most enticing words to keep as essence words for yourself on your journey to financial freedom. They can be a little reminder of what you stand for.

Some of mine are:

Simple
Elegant
Peaceful
Effortless

Whatever *your* essence words are, keeping them in mind will help you build your ideal life based on principles which are important to you.

Link your values with new beliefs

The secret to your financial success is what you take on as your beliefs. This is a really important concept to grasp, because it affects everything. For me, I link fun and pleasure to being thrifty. I like to utilize free or inexpensive options before I go shopping. So, if I want to refresh my current season's wardrobe, I'll go and have a play around and a sort out before looking for new.

It's also helpful to jump into the future for a moment. I feel like I have quite a full wardrobe, so in my mind I step past the fun of buying new things and imagine myself pushing hangers to the side to fit them in. The excitement of something new would be dulled by the overstuffed feeling of too many clothes and not enough space. This little exercise helps me 'want' to shop my closet first, and tidy it up too.

The amazing thing is, by going in and making room for new purchases if that's what my plan is, I sometimes forget about shopping altogether. And this is because I've rediscovered favourite pieces, found others that I bought off-season and had forgotten about, and start putting together new outfits. And, when I do find a gap to be filled, there is that satisfying feeling of shopping with purpose, and coming home feeling content and happy with myself, instead of remorseful.

If you have beliefs when it comes to shopping that you'd like to change, how can you flip them around? Do want to become more resourceful, and less reliant on stores telling you what you 'need'? Do you sometimes feel out of control?

What about telling yourself:

I'm the one in charge of my wallet
I love finding elegant solutions without spending money
I have everything I need already
I love finding free or inexpensive ideas to try
I enjoy the simple and free things in life

Whatever your negative beliefs are about shopping less and using what you have (maybe it sounds boring to be this way?) flip them to the opposite.

'It's too boring to stay home and tidy up my wardrobe' becomes:

I am editing my personal style
I am my own stylist discovering hidden treasures
I am creating my bespoke capsule collection for the season
I am curating my true style
I love being a savvy fashionista

Or, 'My home feels uninteresting and I would like some new décor items to perk things up' becomes:

I love creating my own personalized décor style

I am coming into this home fresh as an interior designer and reworking things

Everything looks best when it is sparkling clean and styled 'just so'

I enjoy taking care of my home and rearranging when I need something new to look at

I love browsing Pinterest in the style I already have, to get fresh ideas on how to arrange things

Try this for yourself; take a list of negative beliefs and flip them around to the opposite, to create your personalized way in which to identify not only what you value, but how your mindset can help you get there too.

Your Financially Chic inspirational ideas:

- What **one belief could you take on** that would be helpful to your financial life, such as mine that it's the best fun to be thrifty?

- **Play around with essence words** which feel the most delicious to you. You don't need to limit yourself to only a few either. I have pages in my journal where I keep adding words as I come up with them and it's so fun to browse that list. It really gets me back in the zone. Use an online thesaurus to find synonyms too; some of my best essence words have been found this way.

- **Create new beliefs** and try them on for size. Soften any resistance by asking yourself, 'How would it feel if I really did believe that I received more pleasure from starting an investment account with $50 a month going into it than spending that same $50 on a new lipstick?' Make it bespoke by including your spending weaknesses and finding something more productive to do with that same money that could also bring you happiness.

Chapter 16.
Your final pep talk

It doesn't matter your age or your financial situation, you can make improvements if you want to. No effort is too small, and it's all worth it!

Believe in yourself and your ability to create a different life if you want to – a life that feels more easeful, wealthier, and full of peace.

Now more than ever it is crucial to get your money ducks in a row, even if in a very simple way. It doesn't have to be complex and you don't have to be fearful of the future, even though things may seem uncertain. I feel it too; I think most people do.

Get a handle on any debt and pay it off. This is the first and most important thing to do in my opinion. Make it an exciting goal to be debt-free and use the tips in this book to help you. It is so important to *shut the door to debt*. Once debt has a foot in the door, watch out! Do *not* welcome debt in; it is not your friend, despite what banks and the colourful advertisements on television say.

A friend who works high up at a major bank once said to us, 'When you don't have debt, you have options', and I've never forgotten that. I have found it to be true, too!

Save and invest in the same way. Make small changes and set up automated investment accounts with the amounts you've saved. *Plant yourself a money tree and watch it grow.* You will probably have heard the old Chinese proverb which says: 'The best time to plant a tree was twenty years ago. The second-best time is now.' And it's the same with your money tree.

An index fund that we started ten years ago, putting in $50 each month has now grown to over $10,000. Once I'd set up the automatic payment I quickly got used to not having that $50 being available to me. I used the 'set it and forget it' principle, and now we have an investment worth more than $10,000. I don't worry about the ups and downs of the sharemarket either, because I know that at times when it's down, I am getting more for my money that month. Everything is on sale!

Just get a handle on debt, save and invest, and **set yourself up for the future** because it's not that hard to do when you start small. But the longer you leave it the worse it will get. And who knows what we'll get thrown at us in the future. I have already seen how we had it 'easy' when my husband lost his job. We didn't have a massive mortgage to pay. We might have had to sell our house if that was the case and how stressful would that have been?

As I said in Chapter 1, I am not a financial expert and none of what I say is intended as financial advice. But I am proof that when you learn to embrace a frugal lifestyle without sacrificing quality or enjoyment, you can find creative ways to live within your means and enjoy life.

Make it fun, make it easy. That's my motto in all aspects of life, and money is no exception. Borrow my faith, borrow my ideas, and create a wealthy and 'rich' life for yourself.

It is possible. You can do it. I believe in you!

With all my best to you for a bright and prosperous future,

Fiona

50 extra tips
to set you on your way
to financial freedom

Welcome to your final 'bonus' chapter. I love finishing my books with a motivating list, and this one was especially fun to write. I thought to myself, *What are my best tips to help you make the most of your money and cultivate an abundant mindset? What would I do if a financial calamity happened and I had to start over? What are some tough love pep talks I've given to myself in the past?*

As you'll know by now from reading through this book, I enjoy making thriftiness into a fun game. I romanticize being savvy with finances and learning how our grandparents lived well on a budget. I also enjoy thinking about the idealized frugality of the traditional European way of living. Food is not wasted, and high-quality clothes are cared for and kept for many years. Good food, culture and fresh air are more valued than shopping malls and online meal orders.

You may be feeling unsettled by the way things are going in the world. You may have just lost your job. You may be facing increased mortgage or home rental payments. You may be living on a fixed income as a retiree. You may be wondering *how you can keep all the plates spinning*.

Start your momentum towards success today. There is no better time to begin than right now. Don't put your financial life on hold; the sooner you start to make changes, the better. And, it doesn't even need to be hard. *Make it easy, make it enjoyable*, and make fun plans for yourself!

I trust you will find this list helpful and get at least a few ideas from it. If there is one that appeals, try it straight away. Let's get cracking!

1. **Don't stress**. Yes, make a plan but don't scare yourself. You need a cool head! Things always seem worse at night when you wake at 2.30am, so write anything down to get it out of your head if you need to and go back to sleep. Breathe deeply and focus on your breaths. Tell yourself it's okay and that you will survive. Ask for answers to come to you in your sleep and try to relax.

2. **Make purchasing decisions slowly** – especially big ones. We only own one car since my husband has had a company car for many years. When he was made redundant, we didn't buy a second car straight away and decided to wait until he had another job to make a decision. Maybe he would get another company car - it just depended on the job. He is now starting a job that does not come with a car but we are still going to wait and see what we want to do. On days that he's at work, I can decide if I want to stay at home, or, if I want to go places, I will drop him to work and pick him up again. I'll probably do this once a week.

3. If you are part of a couple, **be a team with your spouse/partner**. View them as your ally and not your enemy. Talk to them and say you would like to explore doing things differently. Inspire them by sharing your dream of living a carefree, wealthy life with no money worries. Get them on board by painting a picture of how things could be in five years if you make these changes now. Start with your own mindset, ideas and plans, and you might not even have to nag your other half. They will see what you're doing. When I have worked on my own plans, my husband Paul seems to change as well, and I never even mentioned my ideas to him. Not just with money, but with health, motivation, or anything!

4. If single, you get to make autonomous choices. **Dream up the most enticing 'ideal lifestyle'** you could possibly imagine, and see if there are any ways you can start being like that today. Romanticize *everything* and make your life like a movie. When you don't have anyone else to consider, whether you are looking to meet someone or not, you get to be the main character in your own show!

5. **Find inspiration from others** to make it fun to be savvy with your money. Look up the FIRE movement online (FIRE stands for Financial Independence Retire Early). Search for YouTube videos showing how people have paid their mortgage off early. Follow people on social media who are focused on making the most of their money and how they live. You may find like I did that these people really change your mind about frugality and that it can be super-fun.

6. **Don't worry about other people** and what they might think about what you're doing. As already mentioned, they don't have to live with your bank account but *you do*. Forget trying to impress them with what you buy or where you go. You won't look very impressive if you're stressed, anxious and broke. *Impress yourself* by having peace within your money life. Keep your plans in your secret garden. Don't try to

explain it, just do it. And let them be them, you don't need to try and change people.

7. **Make more meals at home**. Once you get into the swing of it you will prefer home-cooked food. Learn how to make your favourites at home. Make burgers and fries on a Friday night. Buy pre-prepared components of meals to start with if that's what it takes for you. If you're used to eating out or buying takeaway food, you may find that the cost of one dinner could supply you with all three meals for the day cost-wise if not more.

8. Make sure you are **getting value from any money you spend**. Look at recurring costs first. If I had to do it, I would cut out all streaming and YouTube Premium. I would take out our home landline. The landline is 'only' $10 a month but everything adds up. When my husband worked I had his shirts laundered because it was quite cheap and they kept the collars white, but now he isn't that cost has been cut naturally. However, I could have taken those back 'in house'.

9. **Never think that a saving is too small**, as long as you don't spend excessive time and money chasing it of course. My brother always used to say to me that he couldn't be bothered using petrol coupons or loyalty cards, and fair

enough, he likes to keep life simple. But for me, if I'm given a 6c/litre petrol voucher with my grocery receipt, why wouldn't I scan it to save $4 when I fill up my car? In my view, every dollar saved is a step towards financial freedom. Every little bit counts!

10. **Project having 'an air of increase'.** Don't think that just because you're cutting back you have to make things plain and austere. Dial it up! Throw an afternoon tea party for your girlfriends at minimal cost and make it a joyous affair. You will have nice things already, I'm sure. Dress up in the clothes you already own, use your best dishes, feel carefree, and make things feel special every day. Wear your beautiful perfumes and makeup. Polish up your lovely sunglasses and *shine* like a movie star.

11. **Use *everything* before you buy more.** Commit to using things up, right to the back of your pantry, or bathroom cabinet. Use shampoo you've pushed to the back, or jarred sauce that's been sitting in your pantry for months. Use cosmetics and toiletries you already own before they go off. Things don't last forever! When you do this, you will find that you had more than you thought you did. And, if it's not a consumable product but you know you are unlikely to use it, donate instead. When you minimize waste, not only do you save money, but you are doing your

bit for the environment as well.

12. **Grow what you eat**. For me I've found the best value and easiest to grow are herbs, spinach, tomatoes, cucumber, and zucchini. Herbs are year-round, and the rest only in the summer. Don't grow difficult things or vegetables you never buy. This is meant to be a money saver/health giver, not an expensive hobby. If you have a small piece of garden, buy a $3 plant and enjoy the benefits. We planted a six-pack of spinach plants because we buy spinach every week for our daily smoothies. The $4 spinach investment fed us for several weeks whereas before we were spending $5-8 a week on bagged fresh spinach.

13. **Make your own French fries** to bake in the oven rather than buying frozen fries. Look at everything you make at home and see if there is a way to do it cheaper. Plus, it's better – healthier *and* yummier. Think about a high-end restaurant, can you imagine them serving up pre-frozen packaged foods? Of course not! Not only will your changes save you money, but they will elevate the quality of your meals.

14. **Know your nice-to-haves** and your must-haves. The nice-to-haves can wait a while, and you can feel good knowing you are building up your wealth (plus you can look forward to

treating yourself in the future). It feels great to know you can make a difference to your wealth by the choices you make every day, no matter how small. *Everything adds up*, remind yourself of this when you're feeling overwhelmed.

15. **Don't skimp on the important things**. It's tempting to try and wing it with insurance or security, but it's not worth your peace of mind. Some things just cost money and there's nothing we can do about it. When policies come up for renewal, shop around to ensure you are still getting the best deal when it comes to household or car insurance for example. It's quick and easy to do an online quote to check this.

16. Take these hard times as a chance to **dream up a new challenge** for yourself. Yes you're doing as well as you can cutting costs, so why not distract your worried mind and set it in a new direction. Become 'obsessed' with something positive. Go on a health kick. Decide to walk every day for forty-five minutes. Learn a new skill from YouTube. Dust off your sewing machine, and tailor your clothes or sew something new.

17. If you don't mind selling online, **see what you have that you can make some money from**. I don't personally enjoy it, so I don't do it

now, but I have done so in the past with excellent results. I've found that once I get into the groove and have listed a few items I enjoy it more. These days I have little to sell, so I'll donate items instead. But if you can receive money from items you don't want, do that. You might even find consignment stores or auction houses in your local area that you can drop items off at. You might not get much, but it will be better than nothing if you were going to donate that item anyway.

18. **Dwell in a sea of abundance**. Be grateful for what you already have. Actually speak it out loud: *Thank you for my home. Thank you for the clothes I am wearing. Thank you for my family. Thank you for my pets. Thank you for the green view from my office window. Thank you for the books on my shelf. Thank you for my job. Thank you for my paycheck. Thank you for my life!*

19. Come up with twenty ways to **pamper yourself for free**. Mine would be to apply a face mask fifteen minutes before I hop into the shower. I'd also display a selection of perfumes and body creams on a tray to remind me to use them - things I already own but are keeping for 'good'. Choose what you'd most like to experience (feeling luxurious, living a luxury life, or pampering yourself). Create a beautiful

menu and then enjoy indulging, often!

20. **Pause expensive hobbies** or halve them. Instead of doing something every week, do it every two weeks if you don't want to cut it out altogether. Some things you will be fine to not do for a while or even forever, and some you will really miss. If you love your Sunday brunch, do it twice a month instead of weekly. The alternate weeks make your own home brunch and make an occasion of it for yourself. Change your daily coffee to a once-a-week treat on a Friday. When I do things too often they become just what I'm used to, but when they are lessened I appreciate them more, as well as save money.

21. **Cut out all takeaways** and junk foods, ice cream etc. You will miss them and be unhappy to start with, but the next day when you wake up not having ingested the calories or spent the money, you will be happy. You could come through the high inflation times not only wealthier, but healthier and slimmer too. Wouldn't that be cool! And instead of making it a miserable practice, romanticize new habits saying that they are creating *your healthiest, sexiest you* or whatever rings your bell.

22. **Don't buy collectibles**, new books, or whatever your weakness is. Borrow novels from the library, and enjoy seeing cute things without

needing to own them. Appreciate what you already have! Rearrange your collectibles, or play around in your closet and make new outfits. Reappreciate things by re-sorting them, polishing and cleaning them, and laying them out in different arrangements.

23. **Keep a lean fridge and pantry** so that items don't expire or spoil. Eat out of your freezer. Sometimes you might not have your best, most gourmet meal, but it's a nice hearty meal and it's free of cost, plus you have created space – decluttering in effect! Let food and drink stocks dwindle. Make meals from what you have and buy as little as possible from the supermarket each week. Make it a fun game to use up every last ingredient, and create new and inspired meals like this.

24. **Don't spend money going out** such as for concerts, travel, gold class movie theatres, dinner and drinks out. It won't be forever, and at the moment you have more pressing needs. Then, when you do go to something you will really enjoy it rather than have it be an outing you're blasé about because you do it all the time.

25. **Find all the free things to do when you go out**. Walks along the waterfront, browsing in the city (if you can guarantee you won't be tempted), going to museums and exhibitions,

and community events too. Pack a picnic and go to the park, beach or lake. Borrow books from the library. Brainstorm a big list for yourself to shop from. For ideas, look at what you enjoy doing that costs money, and flip it around to find the free option. For example, many years ago my husband and I loved going out for brunch on a Sunday, lingering over coffee and the Sunday papers. As in tip 20 of this list, we decided to save the money and put it towards our house deposit instead by making brunch and coffee at home, and our only expense was walking down to the shop to buy a Sunday paper for ourselves.

26. **Give yourself fun money** – actual cash in your wallet. Let's say you decide on $20 a week. You probably won't want to break the $20 on a magazine whereas before you might have tapped your card without a second thought. The next week you'll have $40, and so on. And, when you do see something you really want, you can buy it for yourself guilt-free.

27. **Keep your drip-feed investments going** if possible, and don't raid your investment funds. Set and forget, and focus on how you can change your spending to improve your financial situation. For most people it can be done. Don't leave yourself short-changed in retirement because you weren't willing to change your ways

now.

28. **Look at a side hustle**, part-time job, or something else additional that 100% of what you earn could go to your financial goals. Do you love browsing eBay? Perhaps you could become an eBay seller. How could you make your hobby and downfall, your saviour and business? Instead of browsing online for new books to buy (I already have a ton on my Kindle!) I can take that same 'happy book' energy and write a chapter. 'Multiple streams of income' is a buzz phrase these days, and anyone can participate by starting their own side hustle.

29. You might feel stretched and victimy but **look at how lucky you are**. Count your blessings, and don't be ungrateful. You have so much more than a lot of other people. Be positive, upbeat, and don't complain or be a victim. Once Paul and I went to view a home for sale, and we went to the wrong house first. There were two for sale right next door to each other and we'd just got mixed up because we didn't realize that. As soon as we walked into the first home, we both went silent. The agent started showing us around, so we just followed along. We thanked him and left soon after saying it wasn't for us, and then saw the actual home we'd come to see was up a driveway next door. We both remember how grim that first house was. It was beautifully

kept, but tiny, cheaply built and not good quality at all. We could tell that quite a few people lived there from the number of beds, and sofas made up as beds. It was a sobering visual that neither of us has forgotten even though it was years ago. It made us see how fortunate we really are.

30. **Take personal responsibility**. You got yourself to where you are now, for better or worse. This is true for all of us. There may have been external factors affecting our circumstances, but it still comes back to us. Instead of complaining about where you have found yourself, choose to feel empowered and take ownership. What you've done in the past has got you here, and what you do from today onwards will steer you in a different direction if you want to. Are you up for the challenge? It could be the making of you if you choose well.

31. **Journal your beautiful future** and *dream*. Pump yourself up. Design your ideal life, read about it, and add to the details often. Create lofty goals for yourself. Inspire yourself by dreaming big. Fantasize your ideal wealthy life and how it might look. Encourage yourself by painting an enticing picture of how things could be in the future. Write down how you want to live in an ideal world. Use Brian Tracy's *magic wand technique* by making a big list of how your life would be if you could wave a magic wand

and have everything be perfect. Let this be your guiding light and your inspiration when you are feeling down, stressed or like you want to blow your money on something dumb. Let your vision remind you of your true desires.

32. **Be more social not less**. Invite neighbours, friends or family around for afternoon tea. Bake a cake if you have the ingredients, or serve cheese and crackers with apple slices and a bowl of almonds. Have a potluck dinner or cook something that everyone would enjoy such as a big *spaghetti bolognese* in the slow cooker served with garlic bread. For the price of a meal out for two you could serve six, including a bottle of wine.

33. **Create a feeling of abundance**. Just because you want to save money, there's no need to feel poor. If you have items around that are broken, make you feel broke, or remind you of your reduced circumstances, get rid of them. If you are using threadbare towels and have better towels in the linen closet, donate the old towels to an animal shelter and use your plush 'too good to use' towels. Declutter to feel rich with what you already own.

34. **Live your rich lady lifestyle**. Brainstorm elegant and luxurious ideas and partake in them. Sip tea with a book or magazine mid-

afternoon. Walk in the sunshine. Visit an art exhibition. Browse the expensive stores in town. Dress up and go out. *Live as if*. Doing both things at once – cutting costs as well as living better – will help you ride out the tough times and maybe even forget about them a little bit since you're enjoying yourself so much!

35. **Think 'elegant' when it comes to your finances**. Elegance doesn't only apply to being graceful and stylish in the way you dress and comport yourself. It can also apply to your lifestyle and your finances with its other meaning of *simplicity* and *effectiveness*. Keep your finances simple, and they will be more effective.

36. **Try a budget at least once**. I have and it helps to write things out just to see where my money is going. But ultimately budgets are not my thing and I am financially successful without being a regular budgeter. However I know people who love putting money into categories and it's really helpful to them. What works better for me is to keep in touch regularly and look at incomings and outgoings once or twice a year just to view the big picture and perhaps make a few changes as a result of what I see. If you do choose to try a budget, list out all your essentials but also find space for fun activities or expenditures too. It will make your budget a

more enjoyable practice if it's not all about practicality. Even if you have very little discretionary income, there has to be room for even a small amount of fun money in order for you to want to 'stick to your budget'.

37. **Give yourself the best chance of success** by focusing on what you want, and being positive and can-do. You are not a victim no matter your financial circumstances. You have choice, and you have empowerment over your own situation. The worst thing you can do is focus on what's bad, being negative, wallowing, and feeling hopeless. Do something, anything, that will help you feel better, even something as small as tidying up your paperwork, shredding old documents, and getting your bank accounts reconciled.

38. **Visit your bank accounts online daily** or at least weekly. Keep an eye on any transactions, and familiarize yourself with your money.

39. **Stay focused on what you can control**. You can't control the government or the general economy but you have control of yourself and your personal economy – how you spend your money, what you do to earn your money, and how you think about money.

40. Download the last twelve months of bank account and credit card transactions to **identify where you are spending your money**. Group your outgoings into categories such as groceries, fuel, housing costs, clothing, toiletries, books, hobbies, and whatever else you spend your money on. Add up your grocery spending and divide by 52 to see what you're spending on average each week. Does it shock you? What about takeaways and dining out? Going out for drinks or brunch? Coffee? It's sometimes shocking how much things add up that you don't realize. Look at all spending objectively as if you were helping someone else with their budget and spending and see where they could trim costs without impacting their lifestyle too much.

41. While you're browsing your twelve months of spending, **look at the one-offs**. Is there something you 'had' to have at the time which was 'only' $99, but it's just sitting there not bringing any value into your life? By looking at the one-offs, you might be inspired in the future not to purchase such items and instead wait a few days to let the impulse slide away. My friend Stephanie writes down anything impulsive she wants to buy, and at the end of the month revisits that list. Often she doesn't want anything on it! And if she does, it might be just one item. The others were likely temporary

desires that didn't align with her long-term goals. Delaying immediate purchases can prevent impulse spending and promote mindful consumption.

42. **Write your goals down** and re-read them often. It will be easier for you to resist impulse purchases when you remember your exciting goal of having your mortgage paid off and zero financial stress. Or to be prepared for a rainy day, or the holiday season without anxiety because you have money in the bank to cover gifts, get-togethers, and even a new outfit. To have paid of all debt whatsoever so that your entire paycheck can go towards living costs and investments. These are all worthy goals! Write down *What it would look like for you to be completely financially free*, and then list all the amazing side benefits you would receive from achieving this.

43. **Choose to live 'well'** within your means. Make a decision that you will thrive in all areas of your life regardless of your income. Cultivate rich friendships by seeking out likeminded people and being interested in them. Appreciate the beauty of nature that is available to you everyday for *free*. Foster an air of positivity and exuberance.

44. **Focus on high ROI activities**. ROI stands for 'return on investment' and is a commonly used business term. What if you thought about the ROI in your financial life, your personal life, and at work, by simply asking yourself at any given time, 'What is going to give me the best ROI right now?' For me, it is writing this chapter, not seeing what's happening on Reddit. In the kitchen it might be choosing a more nutritious meal option. In your closet it would mean choosing the clothing items to wear that day which makes you feel your best. And with money, it might be seeing a magazine on the bookstore shelf, choosing to read it instead from the library on your iPad, and to take it a step further, transfer the magazine cost to your savings account. Even $10 can make a difference over time. It's fun to make use of this term, and I don't think there would be a single area in your life in which it couldn't apply to!

45. **Create value**. Differentiate yourself from others by being efficient and productive. At work, focus on working while you are there, and not so much on socializing or chit chat. I do this in my office too. I try to make my time at the keyboard count. And when I do find my mind wandering, I use Brian Tracy's mantra 'Back to work'. *I've got to get back to work*. It really works too! My husband and I use it when we have a mid-morning coffee break. When we've

finished we say 'Back to work!' and we both go our separate ways to whatever we were doing before.

46. **Embrace change** by welcoming rather than resisting whatever you are going through right now. You may not like to hear this, but the situation will still be the same regardless of which mindset you decide on. By choosing to be welcoming, resistance will dissolve away, leaving you with a clear mind able to make helpful decisions, and maybe even a hint of sunshine peeking out from behind the clouds. Wishing for things to be different will not help at all (if it did I'd tell you to go for it!)

47. **Be a continuous learner**. Don't just 'get through' the current economic times, have it be the start of a new direction for yourself. Find books on money that resonate with you (*The Latte Factor* by David Bach is a book I enjoyed, it's a story with a message. I love it when inspirational concepts are woven through a fiction book!)

48. **Cultivate inexpensive hobbies** which will enrich your life, such as gardening, painting a room in your home, sewing clothes or doing your own tailoring and mending, creating artwork on inexpensive canvas with acrylic paints, sketching fashion illustration, birds,

nature scenes or even Parisian vistas from photographs on art paper with watercolour pencils. You may even learn new skills which will enable you to be more self-sufficient and less reliant on expensive services. It might not be the best fun in the world to hem a pair of jeans, but when I've done them there is a feeling of satisfaction, not only for the $20 saved, but a job well done.

49. When you do need to replace something necessary, do your research and **buy the best quality you can afford at the time**. Cut out the 'junk spending', and invest in items which will bring you long term value. If you go forward like this you will save money in the long run.

50. **Celebrate financial milestones**. As you make progress, even if small, acknowledge it. Whether it's paying off debt, starting a savings or investment account, or cutting costs while increasing your standard of living, cheer for yourself. It's all the little changes as well as any big ones that will get you to where you are going. As long as you are heading in the right direction you have reason to celebrate!

To Finish

Thank you so much for reading *Financially Chic Vol. 2: How to be savvy with money in tough times, cultivate your rich lady lifestyle, and live fabulously for less.*

I sincerely hope you gained inspiration from these pages as well as encouragement to feel differently about money and finances: more positive, uplifted, and inspired. It is my goal to try and help everyone see money in a new way. A way that is exciting and fun, not scary and heavy. I sincerely hope that this book has done that for you.

If you have a moment, I would be beyond grateful if you could leave me a review on Amazon. Even a few words are perfect – you don't have to write a lot. A review is the best compliment you can give to an author. It helps others like yourself find my books, and I'd love to get my message of living well through an inspired mindset to as many people as possible.

And if you have a friend who you think would enjoy this book, please tell them about it, or loan them your copy if you ordered the physical book. Did you know that most libraries welcome suggestions on what to purchase? Maybe you might like to suggest this book for your local public library. That way, lots more people can read it!

If you have anything you'd like to say to me personally, please feel free to write:

fiona@howtobechic.com

Maybe you have a book idea for me, want to let me know what you thought of this book, or have even spotted an error. I hope not, but if you do find a typo, please let me know!

Think of me as your friend all the way down in New Zealand wishing you well. I am cheering you on to handle your money better than ever, to thrive financially, feel more abundant, and try new creative projects that might even bring in some cash.

No matter our age, we can always try something new, something different. It's never too late for fresh inspiration. If we're still breathing, we have the whole world spread out in front of us.

With all my best to you, and I look forward to seeing you in my next book!

Fiona

PS. If you enjoyed this book, check out two of my other titles which are on similar topics:

Financially Chic: Live a luxurious life on a budget, learn to love managing money, and grow your wealth

100 Ways to Live a Luxurious Life on a Budget

About the Author

Fiona Ferris lives in the beautiful and sunny wine region of Hawke's Bay, New Zealand, with her husband, Paul, and their rescue pets.

She loves to write about living a fabulous life, chic self-development and cultivating a feminine personal style. Fiona is passionate about the topic of living well, in particular that a simple and beautiful life can be achieved without spending a lot of money.

Her books are published in five languages currently: English, Spanish, Russian, Lithuanian and Vietnamese. She also runs an online home study program for aspiring non-fiction authors.

You can find Fiona's other books at:
amazon.com/author/fionaferris

And connect with her at:

howtobechic.com
fionaferris.com
facebook.com/fionaferrisauthor
twitter.com/fiona_ferris
instagram.com/fionaferrisnz
youtube.com/fionaferris

Other books by Fiona Ferris

Thirty Chic Days: *Practical inspiration for a beautiful life*

Thirty More Chic Days: *Creating an inspired mindset for a magical life*

Thirty Chic Days Vol. 3: *Nurturing a happy relationship, staying youthful, being your best self, and having a ton of fun at the same time*

Thirty Slim Days: *Create your slender and healthy life in a fun and enjoyable way*

Financially Chic: *Live a luxurious life on a budget, learn to love managing money, and grow your wealth*

How to be Chic in the Winter: *Living slim, happy and stylish during the cold season*

How to be Chic in the Summer: *Living well, keeping your cool and dressing stylishly when it's warm outside*

A Chic and Simple Christmas: *Celebrate the holiday season with ease and grace*

The Original 30 Chic Days Blog Series: *Be inspired by the online series that started it all*

30 Chic Days at Home: *Self-care tips for when you have to stay at home, or any other time when life is challenging*

30 Chic Days at Home Vol. 2: *Creating a serene spa-like ambience in your home for soothing peace and relaxation*

The Chic Author: *Create your dream career and lifestyle, writing and self-publishing non-fiction books*

The Chic Closet*: Inspired ideas to develop your personal style, fall in love with your wardrobe, and bring back the joy in dressing yourself*

The Peaceful Life*: Slowing down, choosing happiness, nurturing your feminine self, and finding sanctuary in your home*

Loving Your Epic Small Life: Thriving in your own style, being happy at home, and the art of exquisite self-care

The Glam Life: Uplevel everything in a fun way using glamour as your filter to the world

100 Ways to Live a Luxurious Life on a Budget

100 Ways to Declutter Your Home

100 Ways to Live a European Inspired Life

100 Ways to Enjoy Self-Care for Gentle Wellbeing and a Healthy Body Image

100 Ways to be That Girl

100 Ways to Be a Chic Success and Create Your Dream Life

100 Ways to Live a Soft, Calm Life

*Go to **www.fionaferris.com** to see books released since this edition was published.*

Receive my email newsletter

If you'd like a little more Fiona in your life, you are welcome to join at the link below to receive my weekly emails of what I've been up to, plus I'll let you know whenever I release a new book.

http://eepurl.com/ggiYoX

Even though my books are on different topics, their common thread is that they are all about living a fab life without spending a lot of money. Plus, setting up your mindset to assist, because everything is easier and more enjoyable then.

~~

And, if you've ever dreamed of being an author, even just a little bit, I offer a ten-part email mini-course. You can sign up at the link below and immediately start to receive writing prompts and tips, and encouragement to write. It's free and it's fun, and it won't take you long to explore just how easy and enjoyable it is to get into the writing flow.

http://eepurl.com/cokN39

Printed in Great Britain
by Amazon